Prof. Dr. Riyadh Tariq Kadhim Al-Ameedi

Causality in English

Anchor Academic
Publishing

Al-Ameedi, Riyadh Tariq Kadhim: Causality in English, Hamburg, Anchor Academic Publishing 2017

Buch-ISBN: 978-3-96067-157-2
PDF-eBook-ISBN: 978-3-96067-657-7
Druck/Herstellung: Anchor Academic Publishing, Hamburg, 2017

Bibliografische Information der Deutschen Nationalbibliothek:
Die Deutsche Nationalbibliothek verzeichnet diese Publikation in der Deutschen
Nationalbibliografie; detaillierte bibliografische Daten sind im Internet über
http://dnb.d-nb.de abrufbar.

Bibliographical Information of the German National Library:
The German National Library lists this publication in the German National Bibliography.
Detailed bibliographic data can be found at: http://dnb.d-nb.de

© Anchor Academic Publishing, Imprint der Diplomica Verlag GmbH
Hermannstal 119k, 22119 Hamburg
http://www.diplomica-verlag.de, Hamburg 2017
Printed in Germany

In The Name Of God

The Merciful, The Compassionate

Dedicated To

The Memory Of My Brother,

The Martyr, IMAD

And To

My Wife

ACKNOWLEDGMENTS

To my supervisor Mr. Firas A. Maroof, I owe a special debt of gratitude. He has much to be thanked for invaluable supervision, constructive suggestions, and sincere encouragement are a few of them. I am particularly grateful to him for encouraging me to tackle this challenging topic in the first place.

I must record my gratitude to all the members of my family for their constant support.

PREFACE

The expression of causality is a universal feature of language. English makes use of certain structures and conjunctions to express it. This study is an attempt to describe and examine the syntactic and semantic aspects of adverbial clauses and phrases of reason through which English expresses causality mainly. The framework of the thesis is systematically embodied in five chapters.

Chapter One is an introduction which specifies the nature of the problem investigated, the hypothesis, purpose, limitation, and value of the study. It also gives an outline of the procedures adopted.

Chapter Two presents the general points of causality as a philosophical concept. The relation of such concept with relevant ideas of language is demonstrated too. The purpose of the chapter is primarily to give a general background concerning the universal nature of causality along with the views expressed by different philosophers with regard to the semantic and logical relations implicit in structures denoting causality.

Chapter Three is a short review of what has been sketched on causality in pre-transformational grammar. It surveys the contribution of traditional and structural grammars in the subject under 'investigation. The traditional treatment of causality has revealed the great wealth of causal relations with other concepts such as adjunct, disjunct, conjunct, time, purpose, result, and concession. The chapter has arrived at the conclusion that phrases of reason are, on certain instances, more concise than clauses. It ends with the analysis of the theory of immediate constituents, the major contribution of structural grammarians in the field of syntax. The chapter has shown clearly how the method is inadequate because it makes no distinction between clauses of reason and any other clauses, and it does not account for the variety of meanings, functions, and positions that a clause may assume in a sentence.

Chapter Four deals with the English adverbial clauses and phrases of reason within the framework of transformational grammar. Since the meanings indicated by clauses and phrases of reason are almost identical, some tentative transformational rules which link these clauses and phrases (surface structures) to the same deep structure are suggested. In other words, these rules may transform a kernel sentence into an adverbial clause and phrase of reason having the same meaning and embed the clause or phrase within a matrix sentence. Before the application of any transformational rule, certain preconditions or structural analyses have to be observed because it may or may not be possible to apply pending on the structural description of the kernel sentence. It has been found out that the transformation is carried out on the adverbial clause. The subject noun phrase of the embedded sentence is deleted if it is the same as that of the subordinate sentence. Otherwise, it is retained with certain restrictions. Some adjectives are nominalized throughout the transformation. Attributive adjectives are reordered with the nouns they modify. The ending of the first word of the verb phrase must be -ing.

A summary of the investigation carried out in the four chapters is introduced in Chapter Five. Besides, some concluding points arrived at throughout the study are outlined along with recommendations for further research in related areas.

LIST OF CONTENTS

CHAPTER ONE

CHAPTER TWO

CHAPTER THREE

CHAPTER FOUR

CHAPTER FIVE

LIST OF ABBREVIATIONS

Adj	Adjective
Adv (P)	Adverb (phrase)
Aux	Auxiliary
Comp	Complement
Conj	Conjunction
Det	Determiner
Inf	Infinitive
MV	Main verb
Neg	Negative
Nom. suf	Nominalizing suffix
NP	Noun phrase
Poss. pron	Possessive pronoun
Pred	Predicate
S	Sentence
Sub	Subordinator
T.adv.cl	Adverbial clause transformation
Tns	Tense
T.pcpl.ph	Participial phrase transformation
V	Verb
VP	Verb phrase
#	Sentence boundary
*	Unacceptable structure
$\longrightarrow$	may be rewritten as

➡	is transformed into
( )	Optionally chosen constituents
⎰ ⎱	Alternatively chosen constituents
[ ]	Contingent alternative chosen constituents

LIST OF DIAGRAMS

CHAPTER ONE

1. Introduction

1.1 The Problem

Causality states that the event or state of affairs in the subordinate clause describes or accounts for the event or state of affairs in the main clause. Adverbial clauses of cause or reason explain the cause of or reason for the action expressed by the verb in the main clause. They are most commonly introduced by the subordinators **because** and **since**:

1.   **I work hard <u>because</u> I want to live better.**
2.   **<u>Since</u> I was not invited, I did not go to the party.**

Matrix and subordinate clauses of reason have certain relationships such that the activity in the former follows temporally that in the latter. Some philosophers believe that the connection between the cause and its result or effect is so necessary that an effect must have happened if a cause has happened.

In spite of their similarities in meaning, some subordinate clauses are ungrammatical when introduced by certain subordinators at certain positions. For instance, each of the following sentence pairs has one grammatical member and an ungrammatical one:

3.   a.   **Because he did not get enough sleep, he was tired.**
    *b.   **For he did not got enough sleep, he was tired.**

4.   a.   **It was because he was nervous that he left.**
    * b.   **It was since he was nervous that he left.**

The difference between a clause introduced by **because** and one beginning with other subordinators like **since** and **as** is that in the former (which usually comes second) the emphasis is on the subordinate clause while in the latter (which usually comes first) the emphasis is on the matrix clause. Moreover, this positional difference reflects a syntactic difference; **'because clauses'** are close to adjuncts whereas **'since clauses'** are more like disjuncts. This is obvious in the ability of **'because clauses'** but not of **'since clauses'** to be the focus of cleft sentences as in (4) above. Yet, a final 'because clause' sometimes functions as a disjunct of reason:

5. **She has lit a fire, because I can see the smoke.**

Adverbials of reason may be related to adverbials of purpose which indicate the purpose of the activity of the main verb. Purpose adverbials are introduced by **so that**, **in order that**, **lest**, and others:

6. **The mother worked all the time so that her daughter**
   should be free for study.

The question: **(Why are you studying English?)** can he answered in the following different ways:

7.   **a . I am studying English because I like it. (reason)**
       b. I am studying English so that I can become
          a teacher of English. (purpose)

Similarly, in:

8.   **He sold the watch to save money.**
The adverbial above can be seen as indicating his purpose in selling the watch and equally his reason for selling it.

Other clauses which can be compared and contrasted with clauses of reason include time, result, and concession. For illustration, the subordinator <u>as</u> indicates reason in (9) and time in (10):

9. **As she had a headache, she went home early.**

10. **The policemen stopped the thief as he was about to enter.**

In the same manner, <u>as</u> and <u>since</u> are conjunctions of time as well as of reason. This dual function may imply ambiguity:

11. **As she was sitting in the garden, she could watch the**

    play on the T V.

    (Since she was sitting in the garden ……… or

    While she was sitting in the garden...)

Causality in English can be expressed, with a number of structures as the following examples illustrate:

12. **The student did not come because he was ill.**

13. **The student did not come because ofhis illness.**

14. **The student did not come on accountof his illness.**

15. **The student being ill, did not come.**

These sentences, obviously, have the same deep structure but different surface structures. Each sentence is derived from two sentences conjoined by a subordinator.

Since English has such complexities in the structures and uses of adverbial of reason and since English adverbials manifest this wide variety of forms, functions, and distributions, there is reasonable justification to carry out the present study.

1.2 The Hypothesis

It is hypothesized that although the expression of reason is a universal feature of language, each individual language makes use of certain structures and conjunctions to express it. English expresses causality mainly through clauses and phrases which, though different on the surface level, are transformationally related to the same deep structure.

1.3 The Purpose

This study aims at presenting the adverbials of reason in English in such a way that it makes, as possible as we could, a full account of them. It is hoped also to arrive at certain suggestions and recommendations that may be of use in the teaching and learning of English reason adverbials.

1.4 The Limitation

English adverbials of reason will be syntactically and semantically viewed. The investigation will touch upon the use of adverbials in positive, negative, and interrogative constructions in English. The distribution of adverbials of reason and the way they fit into patterns will be investigated as, far as their occurrences and relations with other adverbials are concerned. The distribution of these adverbials in forming different types of sentences will be investigated too.

1.5 The Procedure

The procedures to be followed in this study may be summed up as follows:

1. Presenting an adequate description of reason adverbials in English and identifying their semantic and syntactic functions and distributions relying on the literature available. Data will be gathered mainly from grammar books but attempt a will be made to subject the data to more recent methods of language analysis, particularly that of generative transformational grammar.

2. Showing the difference?! between clauses of reason and others, especially those of purpose and time.

3. Introducing tentative rules to show the deep structure underlying clauses and phrases of reason.

1.6 The Value

The investigation will be valuable in Its theoretical respect mainly. It will present an up-to-date picture of adverbial clauses and phrases of reason in English. It is also hoped to give a better insight to teachers, curriculum designers and text book writers about the nature of problems involved in the learning and teaching of such clauses.

CHAPTER TWO

2. Causality in Philosophy (Semantic Analysis)

2.1 Some Introductory Remarks

It is held that "science without philosophy is blind while philosophy without science is empty." The present chapter is devoted to a study, however brief, of the general points of causality as a philosophical concept. The need for such a study arises from the fact that it will provide a general background for the subsequent chapters. The account of the subject will not be so detailed to the extent that it will result in complexity.

2.2 The Familiar Idea of a Cause

The topic of causality is the field of a fierce struggle among philosophers all over the world. Here are some of the familiar opinion of causality.

2.2.1 The Universal Aspects of Causality

The notion of causality, as seen by Stace (1962 : 6), is the foundation of all sciences except the purely mathematic ones. Every science assumes the truth of the law of causation, which will shortly be discussed. Each is concerned with discovering the causes or reasons or principles underlying the activity of its special subject matter. For example, in ethics, one asks what causes the good life: in politics what causes the good slate; in medicine what onuses disease; in language what causes acceptable or grammatical sentences and so on. Thus, the notion of causality is not only absolutely essential In common affaire of life but also in all applied sciences.

Thus, as Russell (1970 : 120) demonstrates, causality is deeply embedded in language and common sense. We say that governments build schools and make roads: to **build** and to **make** are both notions requiring causality.

Similarly, we ask :

'Why does the baker make bread ?' and

'Why are railways built ?'

The answers might be:

'Because people will be hungry.' and

'Because people wish to travel' respectively.

Logically speaking, the subordinate clause in such causal statements or propositions assigns the cause of or reason for what is asserted in the main clause. The usual signs are **because, for**, and **since**. For example:

1. **Because they fail to see the purpose of human existence, their lives are meaningless.**
2. **Pope is genuinely happy for he is truely virtuous.**
3. **Since she is interested in music, she takes the course.**

2.2.2 The Absolute Necessity of Causality

Explanation is a very deep-rooted human tendency. Hutchins (1952: 155-156) states that even philosophers who think that we cannot arrive at knowledge of causes get involved in interpreting why this is so. Nor will their arguments and discussions about theory of causes ever remove the word **because** from their vocabularies of common speech. Tolostoy says: "the impulse to seek causes…is innate in the soul of man."

All the questions are answered except the question "Why ?" Dante is of the opinion that man sometimes must be content with the knowledge of something without knowing why. Virgil writes "Happy the man who has been able to know the causes of things."

2.2.3 Definitions of Causality

Most writers on the subject of causation agree in some way or another in their explanations of causality. For a better understanding of it, it is useful to refer to some of the more common definitions to see how they are alike. Taylor (1967 : 56) states that "a cause has traditionally been thought of as that which produces something and in terms of which that which is produced, its effect, can be explained." Rosenthal and Yudin (1967 : 68) regard causation as a main philosophical category referring "to the necessary connection between two events, one of which, called the cause, determines the other, called the effect or consequence. Likewise, Flew (1979 : 54) considers causation to be the relationship between two events; the first brings about the second:

4. Because the switch is turned on, the light shines.

All these definitions have in common a cause and an effect. In sentences of adverbial clauses of cause, there are main and subordinate clauses. The former is the effect while the latter(s) is (are) the cause(s).

2.2.4 The Different Expressions of Causality

The idea of causality can be expressed with a number of ways. To see how causality, in this sense, operate in language, we cite the following instances from Frank. He (1972 : 248-249) illustrates different structures based on the adverbial clause of cause in the following sentence :

5. Because Mr. Black was an extremely timid person,
he did not try to advance himself professionally.

a. Mr. Black did not try to advance himself professionally for he
was an extremely timid person. (coordinate clause)

b. On account of his extreme timidity, Mr. Black did
   not try to advance himself professionally.
   (prepositional phrase with abstract noun)

c. On account of his being extremely timid, Mr. Black
   did not try to advance himself professionally.
   (prepositional phrase with gerund)

d. Being extremely timid, Mr. Black did not try to
   advance himself professionally.   (participial phrase)

e. Mr. Black, being an extremely timid person not try to
   advance himself professionally. (absolute construction)

f. Mr. Black, who was an extremely timid person, did
   not try to advance himself professionally. (adjective clause)

g. An extremely timid person, Mr. Black did not try
   to advance himself professionally. (appositive noun phrase)

h. Extremely timid, Mr. Black did not try to advance
   himself professionally. (appositive adjective phrase)

In addition to this, a gerund phrase (as in a) or an abstract noun phrase (as in b) functioning as subject may express cause:

6. Because he selflessly devoted himself to his students, he won
   the respect of all.

a. His devoting himself selflessly to his students won
   him the respect of all.

b. His selfless devotion to his students won him the respect of all.

19

2.3 Other Notions of Causality

Philosophers have realized many kinds of causes. Here are some of these causes.

2.3.1 Muslim and Aristotle Doctrines of Causality

Muslim philosophers such as al-Kindi, al-Farabi, Ibn-Sina, Ibn-Rushid, al-Gazali and others have provided us with a highly developed concept of causation and contributed a great deal to the revival of a new field on which philosophy, science and theology stand. In general, the analysis of causality, particularly the Islamic analysis, is based on the existence of God which is the cause of everything. Thus, there is no entry for the word <u>cause</u> in the Encyclopedia of Islam (1966: 1130); instead, it is embedded under the word <u>Allah</u>.

On the other hand, Aristotle, as Stumpf (1983 : 90) remarks, distinguishes four fundamental different sorts of causes to represent a broad framework or pattern for the explanation of everything. These causes are formal, material, efficient and final. Having an object of art, for example, the four causes night be : ''a statue", "of bronze", "by a sculptor", and "for a decoration". Unlike most muslim philosophers, Ibn-Uina (d. 1037), Nasar (1964 : 229-231) claims, does not adopt the doctrine that God is the cause of all things. Rather, he follows the theory of Aristotle of the four causes.

2.3.2 Multiple Causality

An effect may be produced by a number of causes. Hutchins (1952 : 159) holds such notion. One cause may be the essential cause of another which is, in turn, the essential cause of the effect, i.e., which brings the effect into existence by its operation. When two causes are simultaneously related to the same effect, one is called the "principal", the other is the "instrumental" cause. The action of a workman sawing wood is a good illustration. The action of the saw causes a certain shape or form of the wood, but it is instrumental to the action of the principal cause, that is, the operation of the workman using the saw.

In sentences consisting of adverbial clauses or phrases of cause, we can find series of causes particularly in coordinate sentences or compound-complex sentences.

Clauses and phrases of reason are coordinated to give a number of causes for a certain effect such as:

7. **I did not understand what you said because either I was not concentrating or you did not make yourself clear or because of Mio noise.**

8. **The car stopped running either because of a bad fuel pump or because of a defect in the ignition or because it ran out of gas.**

2.3.3 Causes as Conditions

Another notion of cause that Foster (1935 : 244) notes is that some contemporary philosophers like Ayer and Collingwood tend to speak of the causal condition of any change as necessary or sufficient or both for its occurrence. In other words, if any of these conditions had not occurred, the change would not have occurred either.

2.4   Universality and Uniformity of Causation

The universality and uniformity of causation are two completely different principles. One of them could be true without the other's, being true.

2.4.1 Universality

By the universality of causation is meant that no change happens without some cause; in short, every event has a cause. Websters Dictionary (1961 : 350) affirms this point in stating that causation means that nothing happens arbitrarily but always as the result of definite series of causes. Similarly, al-Farabi (d. 950), as cited by Hammond (1947: 16-17), formulates the principle of causality on the basis that every event must have a cause. Such proposition expresses the indispensable dependence of every effect on some cause.

Taylor (1967 : 57) maintains that throughout the history of philosophy and until very recent time, the universality of causation has been considered very obvious and sometime seven self-evident. Today, what was considered quite obvious turns out to be controversial. There are many thinkers and philosophers who claim that some change may result with no cause at all. Flew (1979 : 54), for example, shows that some events at the atomic level do not have causes; they occur at random. Russell confesses that an advanced scientific understanding of the world needs no such notion, i.e., universality of causation. Therefore, Taylor (1967 : 57-58) concludes that there is no philosophical way of proving the universality of causation.

What is more, there is no scientific or empirical way to prove the universality or non-universality of causation since occurrences which seem to constitute exceptions are perfectly common. If some change takes place and no cause of that change is recognized, as often happens, one can say that no such cause exists.

2.4.2 Uniformity

Uniformity of causation means that the relations between changes can be expressed in the form of general laws; in brief, similar causes always produce similar effects. Taylor (1967 : 57-53) states that some philosophers like Hume and Mill express this principle in the statement "the future will resemble the past." That means, the fact that something has happened a number of times makes us expect it to happen again.

This principle, in contrast with that of universality, is relatively recent in philosophy. It emerges with the development of science and its emphasis on the laws of nature. Obviously, there is a close relation between statements expressing causal connection and those expressing laws of nature in the sense that the former eight be explained in terms of the latter.

Barrett (1959: 215-217) points out that uniformity in nature gives the probability that under the same conditions the same results will follow in the future as in the past. We have learned from experience in the past that thunder follows lightning, that the sun rises every morning and the like. Prom such experience, we learn only that general regularity has existed in the past; we do not learn with certainty whether it must be so or it will continue to be so in the future. We cannot know that we hear thunder after seeing lightning nor that the sun will rise tomorrow. Hence, this is a process of assuming rather than proving the uniformity of nature.

As a result, this principle is criticized in that it is always possible to find examples of things behaving according to such a law but which are not causally connected. Russell (1968: 93), for instance, remarks that day is invariably followed by night and this by that and yet neither is the cause of the other. The orthodox response is that day could not be called the cause of night because it would not be succeeded by night if earth's rotation were to cease or to grow so slowly that one total rotation would take a year. A cause is,: thus, not necessarily followed immediately by its effect.

2.5 The Idea of Necessary Connection

It was generally supposed that there is a certain necessary connection between any cause and its effect.

The effect must happen if the cause exists. That is, the cause compels the occurrence of its effect. For instance, if the sun shines upon wet clothes, it is not merely true that the wet clothes become dry but they must become dry.

The first really serious challenge to this approach, as Russell (1948: 960) claims, comes from Hume with whom the modern philosophy of causation starts and about whom Korner (1986: 137) raises the question why philosophers are so keen on Hume's treatment of causality when physicists seem to be happy with the concept of causal law. Stumpf (1983 : 273-274) and Copleston (1964 : 82-92) show how the concept of causality is suspect for Hume. The idea of causality arises in the mind v/hen we experience certain relations between things. The first relation is that of contiguity; objects, whether causes or effects, are always close together. The second relation is of temporal priority; the cause must always precede the effect. The constant conjunction is the third relation; the cause is always succeeded by the effect.

Yet, Hume points out that the idea of any cause is entirely separable in our minds from its effect. In other words, any cause can be imagined without its usual effect or with some effect which never accompanies it. Put another way, there is no inherent connection between a cause and its effect. One event follows another but we can never observe any tie between them. "They seem conjoined, but never connected." (Taylor : 1967 : 58-59).

It has been found out that causes necessitate their effects in a special manner in which the effects can never necessitate their causes. To take the example just mentioned, the sun might shine upon wet clothes and hence makes them dry but in a sense in which it could not be said that the clothes, in becoming dry, makes the sun shine upon them.

This topic, i.e., the necessary connection, in relation to semantic and syntactic clause of cause interpretations, deserves special attention because it has direct hearing on the semantic and syntactic aspects of clauses and phrases of reason. In many sentences of explanation with **because** between clauses, the subordinate clause describes an event or state of affairs which causes the event or state of affairs described in the main clause in the sentence:

9.   **Huda did not lend Ahmed money because he would never**
      pay her back.

the event in the main clause is accounted for by the event in the 'because clause'.

But there are many other explanatory sentences in which, at the level of surface structure, the event or state of affairs in the 'because clause' neither causes nor accounts for the event or state of affairs in the main clause. In the following example :

10.   **Jack is probably sick, because he did not show up for work.**

the fact that Jack did not show up for work does not cause him to (probably) be sick nor does it account for his (probable) sickness in some other way.

In addition to this, sentence (10) is not parallel to sentence (9) in the surface structure if we consider the following. Although the subordinate clause in (9) presents a person1s reason, we also talk more generally of any explanation as the reason for an event or state of affairs. Thus, we can paraphrase (9) as (11):

11.   The reason why Huda did not lend Ahmed money is that he would never pay her back.

But (10) cannot be paraphrased in this way. This shows that the ' because clause' does not explain the event or state of affairs in the main clause:

12.*   The reason why Jack is probably sick is that he did not show up for work.

Morreall (1979 : 231-236) thinks that although sentence (12), at the level of surface structure, does not follow the standard pattern for explanatory sentences using <u>because</u>, we can account for it on the standard pattern if we view the deep structure of its main clause as containing some such phrase as 'I judge that' which indicates that the main clause is an inference which the speaker is making, on the evidence presented in the 'because clause'. The event or state of affairs described in the 'because clause' accounts not for the event or state of affairs in the main clause but for the speaker's judging that the event or state of affairs in the main clause obtains. The subordinate clause presents the speaker's evidence for the judgement which he makes in the main clause. Such use of **because** is called the evidential use of **because**.

In sentence (10), where the speaker's inference is based on reasoning from an effect to its cause, the sentence with the evidential use of **because** is the reverse of the sentence with the causal **because** which would be:

13. Jack did not show up for work because he is probably sick.

The effect "Jack did not show up for work" takes place because of its cause "Jack is probably sick". But in a causal inference we reason backwards, from effect to cause. We deduce that there is a certain cause because of a certain effect. So, (13) presents Jack's probable sickness as the cause, and Jack's not showing up for work as the effect; while (3.0) presents Jack's not showing up for work as the evidence of the inference, and the judgement that Jack is probably sick as what is being inferred.

Sentence (10) could be paraphrased to better bring out its deep structure by adding a judgement phrase to the main clause.

14. I think that Jack is probably sick, because he did not show up

for work.

Now, the same form of explanatory sentence in (9) is applied in (14). The main clause describes an event, the speaker making a certain judgement and the subordinate clause describes another event which prompts his making that judgement. The 'because clause' describes the speaker's evidence for his judging that the event in the main clause obtains, and thus the 'because clause' explains the main clause.

With the expanded form of (14), the common pattern for explanatory sentence 'The reason why ... is that ...' is possible, confirming our intuition that (14) and so (10) in their deep structure , are explanatory sentences. Therefore, (14) and (10) can be paraphrased by (15) just as (9) is paraphrased by (11) :

15. The reason why I think that Jack is probably sick is that he did not show up for work.

Sentence (15) is acceptable whereas (12) is not because (15) makes it clear that the reason involved is the speaker's reason for judging that the event in the main clause obtains while (12) can only be interpreted as providing a reason for the event in the main clause obtaining.

2.6 The Distinction between Cause and Reason

Stace (1962 : 76-77, 268) draws the distinction between cause and reason through the following example of life and death. Death is always due to external causes such as accidents or disease. Ordinarily, while life lasts, it remains life unmixed with death and it goes on being life until something comes from outside in the form of external cause and puts an end to it. If we are able to remove the causes, we could conquer death. The causes of death are commonly disease and accidents. There is no reason why science should not progress so far as to eliminate disease and accidents from life. In such case, life might be made immortal or at least be prolonged. The law of causation admits no exception.

Accordingly, in every case of death, causes precede it. But to give the cause is not to give any reason for an event. Causation tells that the event A is invariably succeeded by the event B and A is the cause of B. This means that whenever B occurs, it occurs in a certain regular order and series of events but it does not tell why B occurs at all.

The reason of a thing, however, has to be distinguished from its cause. The reason of the man's death is not to be found in the causes that bring about his death. The reason is that life is already death potential. Whereas the cause of death is merely the mechanism, by the instrumentality of which, through one set of causes or another, the inevitable end is brought about.

The syntactic and semantic differences between cause and reason are going to be further discussed in the following chapter.

2.7   The Distinction between Cause and Effect

Any proper analysis of causal relation should distinguish between causes and effects analytically, and it should not ignore the differences between them. Taylor (1967 : 64) indicates that an analysis of the statement of the form "A is the cause of B" does not entail that "B is the cause of A" or that it is arbitrary which one considers the cause and which the effect. As a matter of fact, the concepts of cause and effect have different uses, and they are not one and the same concept. Some philosophers particularly Russell and McTaggert suggest that there is no theoretical difference between cause and effect, and it is arbitrary which one calls which.

One of the other differences between a cause and its effect is that of power. A cause acts upon its effect in a manner in which the effect cannot act upon its cause. Put another way, a cause produces its effect in a way that cannot be expressed in terms of the views of necessary and sufficient conditions,(See 2.2.3). Modern philosophers seek to distinguish causes from their effects in terms of temporal considerations.

2.7.1 Cause and Time

Most philosophers agree that causes precede their effects. It was suggested that if the cause always takes place before its effect, there is no need to speak of any special power of the cause in relation to its effect.

In this sense, Poster (1985 : 251-253) signifies that Ayer attempts to build the intuition that the cause must precede, or at least be no later than, the effect into his analysis. He uses the word **cause** in the sense that if one event is said to be the cause of another, it is implied that it precedes, or at any rate does not follow, the event which is said to be the effect.

On the account that the past is fixed and the future is open, we can use the relations of necessity and sufficiency which run in both directions to influence the future but not the past. For Ayer, both past and future are closed in the sense that they cannot be changed and both are open in the sense that they cannot be inferred from the present. The only sense in which the past is closed and the future is open is that present activities can causally influence the future but not the past. This is based on the very principle that causes cannot follow effects. Moreover, we think of the causal processes as moving forwards in time because the past is settled and is thus no longer something on which we could hope to exert an influence.

Anyhow, as far as adverbial clauses of cause or reason are concerned, Quirk et. al (1985 : 1103-1104) demonstrate that we subsume under clauses of reason several types of subordinate clauses that convey basic similarities of relationship to their matrix clauses. There is, for all types, generally a temporal sequence such that the situation in the subordinate clause (i.e., the cause) precedes that of the matrix clause (i.e., the effect).

2.7.2 Contemporaneous Cause and Effect

Richard Taylor (1967 s 65-66) claims that some philosophers like A.E. Taylor and Reid maintain that causes cannot be perfectly conceived except as objects having the power to produce certain changes in other objects. It is this element of power rather than any mere accident of temporal position that distinguishes causes from their effects.

On the other hand, other philosophers such as Taylor and Collingwood point out that causes and effects are contemporaneous. That means, there is never any real temporal succession of events that are causally connected. If this claim is true, the difference between causes and their effects is not a temporal difference. Besides, one cannot distinguish between two events causally connected with each other, which is the cause and which is the effect by asking which happens first in time since neither of them happens first.

An illustration of cause and effect which appear contemporaneous is the following. Consider the relationships between one's hand and a pencil with which one is writing. Obviously, it is the motion of the hand that is the cause of the motion of the pencil and not vice versa. This means that the motion of the hand is sufficient for the motion of the pencil. The motion of the pencil is also sufficient for the motion of the hand. Neither the hand nor the pencil can move without the other's moving with it. In addition, the motion of either is also a necessary condition for the motion of the other. Consequently, the motions are contemporaneous. They move together in a sense that one cannot distinguish cause from effect by any consideration of which occurs first. It is clearly false to say that the hand moves first and then the pencil begins to move. There is no temporal gap at all between cause and effect in this sense.

CHAPTER THREE

3. Traditional Treatments of Causality

3.1 Some Introductory Remarks

This chapter attempts to survey briefly the most general aspects of adverbial clauses and phrases of cause or reason as viewed and analyzed by non-transformational grammars. The survey will subserve as a connecting link between the preceding and following chapters. A significant source to be cited and consulted worth mentioning is going to be **A Comprehensive Grammar of the English Language** by Quirk, R., Greenbaum, S., Leech, G., and Svartrik, J.(1985). The title, authors, and year of the book may justify our consult.

3.2 Causal Linking in English

Causal relationships play an important role in human communication, and they appear in a variety of lexical and grammatical forms whose use and appropriateness are determined by various contextual factors. By studying these forms, we can learn a great deal about the degree of stylistic and functional variation that is possible in this particular area as well about the different discourse strategies the speakers and writers employ. As a starting-point, it is thought better to outline some of the different strategies that a causal relationship may assume.

A causal relation, as stated in chapter two, can be said to exist between two events or states of affairs if one is understood as the cause of or reason for the other. Hossack (1979 : 28-29) thinks that statements like the following:

l. a. Mill played very well. He was chosen with the first team.
have an obvious causal relation. The fact that "Mill played very well" gives the reason for 'yh.is being chosen with the first team". This causal relation can be

shown by a number of words such as: **so**, **therefore**, **on account of this**, **owing to this**, etc.:

    b. Mill played very well. So, he was chosen with the first team.

    c. Mill played very well. On account of this, he was chosen with

      the first team.

But these words although showing the causal relation clearly, cannot link. There are three ways of showing this relation by linking. First, by an adverb clause of cause:

    d. Mill was chosen with the first team because he had played

      very well.

Secondly, by a participial phrase :

    e. Having played very well, Mill was chosen with the first team.

Finally, by a prepositional phrase plus an abstract noun or gerund :

    f. Owing to his good play, Mill was chosen with the first team.

Bartsch (1976 : 3) confirms that the logical analysis of adverbial constructions leads to underlying structures which show how the sentence is understood. For instance, the following sentences have identical logico-semantic structures:

    2. a. John calls the doctor because he is ill.

       b. John calls the doctor because of his illness.

       c. John is ill. Therefore, he calls the doctor.

       d. John is ill. He calls the doctor.

The causal relation is explicitly given by means of a conjunction (a), a preposition (b) and a connective (c). This relation is not made explicit in (d); it can be deduced from context, i.e., from the knowledge of normal behaviour in the society. The second sentence in (d) gives the reason or explanation for the state described in the first sentence.

For Altenberg, this is not the whole story. He (1984 ; 20-21) adds more forms that can express causality. The cause or its result can be encoded as a phrase, a dependent clause, an independent clause or a sentence:

3.a. Because of a car accident, Peter is now in hospital.

b. Peter's accident, resulted in a week in hospital.

c. Peter is in hospital because he had an accident.

d. Peter had an accident,. That's why he is in hospital.

The relationship between the causal members, i.e., the cause and its result, can be signalled either explicitly by means of an overt causal link such as **because of**, **because**, **result in**, and **that's why** in the examples above, or implicitly by juxtaposition or coordination (with or without ellipsis):

e. Peter had an accident. He is now in hospital.

f. Peter had an accident and (he) is now in hospital.

It is noted that the members of the causal relations can be presented in different orders either with the result preceding the cause as in (c) or in the reverse order as in the other examples. A study carried out by Altenberg (1984 : 51-52) shows that the result-cause sequence is slightly more frequent than the cause-result sequence (54% and 45% respectively) while the medial cause in which It can be inserted parenthetically in the member containing the result, as in (4), is very rare (1%):

4. You think, because you are rich, you can buy justice.

In fact, examples (3) and (4) represent only a small sample of the many possible causal expressions in English.

In the light of the above, we note that causal relationships can be expressed in various ways. On the whole, most writers on the subject agree that the relation is chiefly expressed by means of subordinators such as **because**, **since**, **as**, or **for**, which we are going to discuss shortly.

Now, we will deal with other structures and words that imply causative relation. Quirk et. al (1985: 1107) maintain that there are certain structures in which part of the predicate precedes the subordinator as that may function as clauses of cause:

5. Knowing her as I do, J am sure to tell you that she

    will never marry you.

The subordination linkage of cause can be a correlative comparative construction (**too ... to**), (Altenberg (1984: 28-29)):

6. Nevertheless, the grumbles and complaints are too

    frequent to be ignored.

Here, the causal relation is demonstrated by the following paraphrase: Nevertheless, the grumbles and complaints cannot be ignored because they are too frequent.

Infinitives, as seen by many grammarians like Quirk et. al (1985: 1091, 1106), Zandvoort (1977: 11) and Jepson (1939: 140-141), can be used to express the notion of cause:

7. She must be strong to lift that heavy box.

There is a sense of **who** implying cause, (See Nesfield (1947: 43):

8. They should forgive my son who (because he) has never

    committed such a fault before.

Having completed this brief survey of the ways causal relationships are expressed, we can now proceed to a more intensive examination of causal conjunctions and their relations within each other and with other conjunctions.

3.3 Major Cause Subordinators

Adverbial clauses of cause or reason give the cause of or reason for the activity expressed in the main clause. One statement is closely dependent on the other showing its necessary cause. These clauses are most commonly introduced by **because, since, as**, and **for**:

9. **I trust you because you speak the truth.**

10. **Since you are a student, you must do nothing but study.**

11. **As she was a wealthy woman, she lived in a good hotel.**

12. **He doubted her promise for she had frequently lied to him before.**

Some grammarians, like Zandvoort (1977 : 216), C. E. Eckersley and J.M. Eckersley (1963: 339) and Tipping (1961 s 307), add the complex subordinators **seeing that** and **now that**. Others, like Wren and Martin (1985: 285) and Jesperson (1952: 370), include inasmuch as and that among those subordinators presenting adverbial clauses of cause:

13. **Seeing that no one volunteered, I finished the work myself.**

14. **Now that they have the last chance, they play much better than we expect.**

15. **Inasmuch as every effort is being made to improve the financial condition of the company, the term of the loan will be extended.**

16. **The mother was very pleased that her son passed.**

The adverbial clauses of cause mentioned above differ greatly in several respects. Clauses introduced by **because**, for example, mostly follow their main clauses; clauses introduced by other conjunctions tend to precede them. The difference between them is basically a difference in emphasis. The emphasis in the 'because clause' is on the subordinate clause while in the other clauses, it is on the main clause:

17. She walked slowly because she was very tired,

18. As she was very tired, she walked slowly.

Altenberg (1984 : 39-41) carries out a study on the major cause conjunctions and draws an analysis of British English based on a sample of 100-000 words from both the spoken London-Lund Corpus (LLC) and the written Lancaster-Oslo/Bergen Corpus (LOB) for the positions and orders of clauses introduced by the basic subordinators. The results he arrives at are illustrated in Diagram (1) below:

Subordinator	LLC	LOB	Total	Order
because	355	70	425	
initial	4	8	12	CR
medial	4	2	6	–
final	347	60	407	RC
for	0	64	64	RC
since	5	33	38	
initial	2	12	14	CR
medial	1	0	1	–
final	2	21	23	RC
as	7	19	26	
initial	2	9	11	CR
final	5	10	15	RC

Diagram (1) Adverbial Clauses (C: Cause, R: Result)

It is to be noted that the conjunction for is included among these subordinators although it is often classed as a coordinator. It seems that the reason behind this is that its meaning approximates that of the sub- ordinators <u>since</u> and <u>as</u>. Jesperson (1970 : 392) and Tipping (1961 : 314) claim that, historically, <u>for</u> is a subordinating conjunction equivalent to <u>because</u> but now it is generally regarded as a coordinating conjuction, Huddleston (1984 : 383) confirms that it falls at the border line between them and seems to lack the positive properties of both. For Wren and Martin (1985 : 208), it is a subordinator expressing an inference which they call 'illative':

19. Something surely fell in; for I heard a splash.

There is one more conjunction that deserves special attention. The conduction **that**, as Wren and Martin (1985: 218) remark, is now used to express a reason and is equivalent to **because**. For Jesperson (1970 : 389), it chiefly serves to express the psychological reason or motive for a state of mind :

20. I am glad that my brother has visited me.

Adverb clauses introduced by **that** are frequently used to modify adjectives but Roberts (1954 : 325) argues that it is preferable to classify them as clauses of cause. In (20), for instance, the clause 'that my brother has visited me' states the cause of gladness. On the other hand, 'that clause', as Chandra and Singh (1974 s 227) and House and Harman (1950 : 384-385) indicate, is used by modern grammarians instead of -because clause- to introduce nominal clauses:

21. The reason the war has lasted so long was that the Iranian governors refused to cooperate.

22. The reason I admired the soldier was that he was very courageous.

3.3.1 Because and For

Of the major conjunctions used to introduce adverbial clauses of cause, the conjunctions **because** and **for** are usually regarded as synonymous but not necessarily interchangeable. A 'for-clause' has a more restricted use than a 'because clause', or in Tipping's words (1961: 314), it is a "weakened because". One of the syntactic features of **for** as a coordinator that Quirk et. al (1985 : 921-922) mention is that coordinated clauses are sequentially fixed in relation to the other clause and therefore cannot be inverted without producing unacceptable sentences or at least altering the relationships between the clauses. This is not true for most subordinators like **because**:

23. a. *For it was raining, I took my umbrella.

b. Because it was raining, I took my umbrella.

Another difference discussed by Quirk et. al (1985: 922-923) and Greenbaum (1969 : 29) is that whereas coordinators are not preceded by a conjunction, subordinators can usually be preceded by conjunctions. In (24-a), two subordinate clauses are linked by **and** which precedes the second subordinator **because**. By. contrast, in (24-b) the conjunction **for** cannot be preceded by **and** in this way:

24.a. Professor Allen enjoys working with foreign students because he gets the pleasure from helping people and because he learns a lot from them.

b.*Professor Allen enjoys working with foreign students for he gets the pleasure from helping people and for he learns a lot from them.

In addition to these differences, Thomson and Martinet (1973: 54) point out that a 'for clause' cannot be used in answer to a question:

25.a.* Why does he behave so? For he is angry.

b. Why does he behave so? Because he is angry.

Moreover, it cannot be a more repetition of what has been already stated but always includes some new piece of information:

26.a.* She spoke in German. He was angry for she had spoken in German.

b. She spoke in German. He was angry because she had spoken in German.

But

27. He was angry for he did not know German.

is correct; **because** is also possible.

Smith and Wilson (1980 : 39-40) note that it is the fact that coordinate clauses have very limited freedom of movement compared with subordinate clauses, which explains the differential patterns in the above instances as well as the following ones:

28.a.* It was for he was tired that he stayed home.

b. It was because he was tired that he stayed home.

29.a.* Suha, who attended the party for I invited her, is returning today.

b. Suha, who attended the party because I invited her, is returning today.

It has been pointed out by Chander and Ranchan (1986: 4-5) and Hook and Mathews (1956 : 349) that the reason for these restrictions is that a 'for clause' does not tell us why a certain action is performed but merely offers a piece of additional information which helps to explain it. In other words, the reason, proof, or justification introduced by **for** is like an afterthought or a parenthetical statement while **because** introduces a direct reason, i.e., the reason is an essential part of the statement.

3.4 Adjuncts and Disjuncts

From a semantic point of view, adjuncts differ from disjuncts in that the former denote circumstances of the situation in the matrix clause while the latter comment on the style or form of what is said in the matrix clause (style disjuncts) or on its content (content or attitudinal disjuncts). The major difference between them in syntax is that disjuncts are peripheral to the clause to which they are attached. This contrast does not appear in differences in form or position. For illustration, the same subordinator may be used to introduce finite clauses that function as adjuncts and disjuncts and the clauses may be positioned initially or finally in both functions. In the following instances, the conjunction **since** is used to present a temporal adjunct and a reason disjunct clause:

30. a. Since the boys left, we have been relaxing.

b. He took his coat, since it was paining.

Quirk et.al (1985 : 1070-1073) refer to a number of syntactic processes that demonstrate the major differences between adjuncts and disjuncts. These differences will be discussed in more detail in the next chapter.

It is to be noted that disjuncts are of two types: "**style**" and "**content**". The syntactic differences (to be discussed in the following chapter) apply equally to both. Semantically speaking, style disjuncts generally imply a verb of speaking and the subject ' **I** '; they implicitly refer to the circumstances of the speech act while content disjuncts refer to the content of the matrix clause. In the following instances <u>since</u> is used as a content disjunct and a style disjunct respectively:

31.   a. Since you know French, you should be able to

translate the document.

b. Since you seem to know, I saw him with your sister.

Similarly, the 'because clause' is a content disjunct in (32.a) and a style disjunct in (32.b):

32.   a. They like him because he is always helpful.

b. They like him because his friend told me so.

Since two clauses with various syntactic functions can't be coordinated; therefore the two clauses above cannot be coordinated:

c.* They like him because he is always helpful and
because his friend told me so.

3.5 Subordinators and Conjuncts

We have observed that the causal relations can be expressed by means of subordinators like **because**, **since** and conjuncts or as usually called sentence connectors like **therefore**, **accordingly**. Marcus (1977: 187-188) indicates that two kernel sentences can be joined together with little or no change simply by adding a conjunct in front of the second sentence. The meaning of the new construction is influenced by the conjunct used. For example, the following construction parallels the meaning of cause and effect:

33.   a. He was guilty; therefore, he was punished.

Such types of connection can be turned into a sentence having a' matrix clause and an adverbial clause of reason:

b. He was punished because he was guilty.

Gleason (1965: 343) expresses this idea in stating that "nearly synonymous but structurally contrasting constructions" can be made with what he calls 'illatives' like **therefore** and **so** and 'causal connectors' like **because** and **as**. Consequently, we see that the above pair (33 a and b) allows the same clauses to be joined so as to give much the same semantic relationship but with very different formal structures.

However, some writers such as Schuster (1965 : 361) and Roberts (1956 : 219-222) believe that the subordinator is not as shiftable as the conjunct. The former, with its clause, can follow or precede the matrix clause without disturbing the relationship between the two clauses (34). The latter, alone, can be moved to various position within the second sentence pattern (35). But it cannot be transposed with its clause in front of the preceding clause; in this case, the relationship between the two clauses is changed and the conjunct must now refer to some preceding clause (36). The following examples help to make the distinction clear:

34.   a. **He was punished because he was guilty.**

   b.   **Because he was guilty, he was punished.**

35.   a.   **He was guilty; therefore, he was punished.**

   b.   **He was guilty; he, therefore, was punished.**

   c.   **He was guilty; he was punished, therefore.**

36.*   **Therefore, he was punished, he was guilty.**

There are cases in which both the subordinator and the conjunct may occur in one sentence (See Quirk et.al, 1985 : 644-645). Some conjuncts can correlate with certain subordinated of the preceding clauses to reinforce the logical relationship between the parts of a sentence. This results from the fact that a similar logical relationship is affected by both, the subordinator and the conduct. For illustration the subordinates **because** and **seeing that** can be combined in initial subordinate adverbial clauses with optional conducts such as **hence** and **therefore** in the matrix clause. So is since with **then** and **in that case**. It is when we combine both a subordinator and a conjunct in one sentence that we have correlation:

37.　　**Because I have not received any instructions from you, I will, therefore, act as I think best.**

38.　　**Seeing that she had no chance of winning, she consequently pretended she was not trying.**

3.6 Contingency

Quirk et.al (1985 : 484) enumerate a number of chief semantic relations under the "adverbial of contingency". These relations are cause, reason, purpose, result, and concession; Obviously, there are close ties between these adverbial types, and it is on this account that they are embedded under the title 'contingency'.

3.6.1 Cause and Reason

Despite being basically similar, cause and reason can be semantically and stylistically distinguished. Cause is concerned with causation and motivation and is seen as established with some objectivity. By contrast, reason involves a relatively personal and subjective assessment, (Ibid):

39. **He died of cancer. (cause)**

40. **He bought the magazine because of his interest in philosophy. (reason)**

However, both can be expressed by prepositional phrases answering the question why ... ? Among these prepositions are **because of**, **on account of**, **for**, **from**, **out of**, **through**, etc. These are common for cause adjuncts. Examples:

41. He was asked to be the commander on account of his
    military skill.
42. I visited her out of gratitude .
43. Through the carelessness of one man, the battle
    was lost.
44. The child was weak from exposure and lack of food.

There is one other preposition that deserves special attention. Some writers still consider **due to** an adjective and must, therefore, be used in connection with a noun. Its use as an adverb is incorrect. Schibsbye (1965: 164) and Quinn (1963: 123) state that some writers object to the use of **due to** in (45.a) and provide (45.b) as an acceptable alternative:

45.a. **Due to bad results, the experiment has been repeated**
       today.

   b. **Repetition of the experiment today is due to bad results.**

Or, they replace **due to** by **owing to** as in the following instance on the account that **due to** is an adjectival not an adverbial phrase:

45. a. **Due to your not coming, we thought you were ill.**

   b. **Owing to your not coming, we thought you were ill.**

In contrast, Drummond (1975 : 281-282) confirms the fact that **due to**, like **owing to** and **because of**. has become a compound preposition which may introduce an adverbial and is, therefore, considered acceptable.

47.a. **Due   to** ⎤   **the   need   for   teachers   in   Basrah**
       Owing   to ⎬   **University,   Mr.   Hassan   is   going**
       Because ⎦   **there next week.**

   b. **Mr. Hassan's departure is due to a need for teachers**
      in Basrah University.

3.6.2 Reason and Purpose

The close link between reason and purpose adverbs arises from the fact that the same question form may be used for both. In other words, we use questions with <u>why</u> and answers with <u>because</u> or <u>so that</u> as well as infinitive expressing purpose. For example, the following question can be answered in different ways:

48. Why does the teacher speak to the class slowly and simply ?

    a.   **The teacher speaks to the class slowly and simply**
            because he wants to make the whole thing clear*

    b.   **The teacher speaks to the class slowly and simply**
            so that he might make the whole thing clear.

    c.   **The teacher speaks to the class slowly and simply**
            to make the whole thing clear.

It is noted that the purpose answers (b and c) can indicate the teacher's purpose in speaking to the class slowly and simply and equally his reason for speaking that way. (See 4.5).

The difference between the two adverbials, Hossack (1979 : 30) states, is that purpose implies deliberate action whereas reason does not.

Because of the close connection between the semantic categories of reason and purpose, the same item may be used for the semantic relation. In this sense, Kench (1981 : 50) remarks that the conjunction **for** can indicate reason and purpose adjuncts:

49. What does she want a hand cream for ? (reason)

50. She will do anything for money, (to get money)

What is more, the negative purpose clause expressed by the conjunction **lest** is closely related to reason clause:

51. I am telling you this lest you might make a mistake.

52. **I am telling you this because you might make a mistake.**

53. **He kept his wife's jewels in the bank lest the house might be burgled.**

54. **He kept his wife's jewels in the bank because the house might be burgled.**

3.6.3 Reason and Result

Another relationship with which grammarians have been concerned is that of reason and result. Quirk et.al (1972: 754), Frank (1972: 250) and Allen (1971: 342) agree that the same cause-effect relationship can often be established in either the cause clause or the result clause. The latter is like an inversion of the former in the sense that the same meaning can be expressed by reversing the subordinate and matrix clause relations and using a subordinator of cause, (See pp. 83-84):

55. **It was quite windy, so that they had to button their coats up.**

56. **They had to button their coats up because it was quite windy.**

57. **Mrs. Allen wants to help her husband, so that she arranges social evenings.**

58. **Mrs. Allen arranges social evenings because she wants to help her husband.**

Yet, there is a syntactic difference between reason and result clauses in that reason clauses are adjuncts while result clauses are disjuncts; thus only the former can form the focus of a cleft sentence:

59. **It was because it was quite windy that they had to button their coats up.**

60. *** It was so that it was quite windy that they had to button their coats up.**

47

3.6.4 Reason and Concession

Concession can be seen as a blocked or inoperative cause. Tregidge (1981 : 160-162) signifies the relation between the two clauses as follows:

61.   a. As she saw the mouse, she screamed.

62.   a. Although she saw the mouse, she did not scream.

It is clear that **as** and **although** are like opposites. 'As clauses', of reason, can sometimes be expressed simply by **-ing:**

61.   b. Seeing the mouse, she screamed.

'Although clauses', of concession, on the other hand, can also be expressed in the same way but in this case the subordinator **<u>although</u>** cannot be omitted:

62.   b. Although seeing the mouse, she did not scream.

Likewise, phrases of reason and concession are like opposites:

63.   Zeki passed because of his test results.

64.   Zeki passed in spite of his test results.

Sentence (63) implies that Zeki's results are good; sentence (64) implies that they are bad.

3.7 Cause and Temporal

Generally speaking, there is a temporal sequence in the causal relationships such that the situation in the subordinate clause precedes in time that of the matrix clause. (See 2.6.1). Some subordinators have multiple uses and the type of clause they introduce can be determined only by an examination of the function of the clause. Yet, Huddleston (1984 : 223) affirms that the distinction is more semantic than strictly syntactic. A look at some of these conjunctions will illustrate this point.

The conjunction **as** can express both time and reason:

65. I met him as I was leaving the hospital. (time)

66. As he is very forgetful, his wife takes care of the details. (reason)

Quirk et.al (1985: 1105) note that this dual function can give rise to ambiguity. For example, as in each of the following sentences can imply **because** and **while** simultaneously:

67. As Alexander designed the engine, he must have realized its great capabilities.

68. As the rain was falling, they sang beautiful songs.

Thomson and Martinet (1973 : 56) express this difference in another way. In their opinion, 'as time' is chiefly used with verbs of doing' and 'becoming' rather than verbs of 'being'. Accordingly, it is not normally used with auxiliary verbs or with verbs of 'emotion' or 'sense' or with verbs of 'knowing' and 'understanding'. If used incorrectly, 'as time' will inevitably be confused with 'as reason'.

On the other hand, as plus a noun could only mean either time (when) or cause (because), i.e., no ambiguity is possible.

69. "As a student, he had lived on bread and water."

(When he was a student, ...)

70. As. an old customer, he has a right to better treatment than that.

(Because he is an old customer, ...)

Another conjunction used to express cause and temporal is **since**:

71. We have been friends since we were children. (time)

72. We wanted them to meet tonight since tomorrow is likely to be too late. (cause)

Wren and Martin (1985 : 217) suggest that **since**, when used in a temporal sense, should be preceded by the present perfect aspect. However, Tipping (1961: 276) states that **since**, when used in the sense of cause , may be used without restriction to tense.

In addition to these conjunctions, Zandvoort (1977: 216) introduces **now that** to combine reason with temporal meaning:

73. **Now that he does it,! I remember. (time)**
74. **Now that he inherited his father's fortune, he does not have to work anymore. (cause)**

The conjunction may indicate simultaneity:

75. **They are happy now that everybody is present.**
76. **Now that she could drive, she feels independent.**

As long as is another conjunction used to mean cause and temporal. Frank (1972: 247) labels it as a synonym for **since**. It Is a more casual conjunction often suggesting the feeling of **anyhow**:

77. **One must be careful as long as he crosses street . (time)**
78. **As long as you are here (anyhow), tell us what happened. (cause)**

Since as long as can also express time, its use may result in ambiguity:

79. **I'll take care of her as long as she is my wife.**
80. **The responsibility falls on my shoulder as long as their father is abroad.**

Some conjunctions like **when**, **while**, **once**, and **often**, usually associated with clauses of time, sometimes introduce clauses with some causal meanings, (See Roberts, 1954: 326):

81. **When you become a member, you will receive a membership card and a badge. (time)**
82. **How can you expect pupils to be honest when you yourself deceive. (cause)**
83. **She wrote her greatest novel while she was living in Spain. (time)**

84. While you are in the library, borrow me the book. (cause)

85. Once you have made a promise, you should keep it. (time)

86. Once he has been proved a liar, he cannot expect others to believe him. (cause)

87. They washed their hands after they have finished eating. (time)

88. I think I will have to bring her a watch, after I said I would. (cause)

However, the relationship between time and reason can be expressed by means of -ing causes without a subject in such a case, Quirk et.al (1972 : 762) point out that a contingency is implied and it is to be inferred from the context. Contingency may be interpreted, according to context, as a causal or temporal connection. In –ing clauses, 'dynamic verbs' such as **ask**, **eat**, **play** typically suggest a temporal link, and 'stative verbs' like **see**, **know**, **love**, a causal link:

89. Reaching the town late, I looked for a hotel (When I reached the town late, …)

90. Living abroad, I had Improved my pronunciation. (Because I lived abroad, …)

Indeed, phrases of time formed with a participle have usually an implication of cause as well, (See 4.4).

91. The ladies having left the room, the men began to smoke.

   a. After the ladies had left the room …

   b. As the ladies had left the room ...

92. The weather having improved, they enjoy the remainder of the match.

   a. After the weather had improved ...

   b. As the weather had improved ...

3.8 Words Compression by Shorter Constructions

At this station, we try to show how variety is essential. Pew writers are very economical in their uses of construction. Thus, a passage can be reduced to two thirds of its original length by various methods such as by reducing clauses to phrases (93) or even, when possible, to single words (94) and by avoiding overuses of some conjunctions (95 and 96):

93. As he was poor, he could not buy that car.

    a. Being poor, he could not buy that car.

    b. Owing to poverty, he could not buy that car.

94 .   **a. They left because they were disgusted.**

    b. They left disgusted.

95. a. They called a mediator because they hoped to settle their differences.

    b. Hoping to settle their differences, they called a mediator.

96 .   **a. Since the directions confused me, I could not attend the 7:15 p.m. meeting.**

    b. Confused by the directions, I could not attend the 7:15 p.m. meeting.

Campbell (1962: 72-73) demonstrates this idea and arrives at the conclusion that phrases are, on many occasions, more concise than clauses. He takes a paragraph of three sentences like the following:

97 .   **a. The man who lives in the house beside yours knew I was ill. He came many times to see me.**

    He wanted to ask if there was anything he could do for me.

Later, these sentences are joined by conjunctions:

b. Because he knew I was ill, the man who lives in the house beside yours came many times so that he might ask If there was anything he could do for me .

This seems better but it is still too heavy. Here, there is a complex sentence of one matrix clause and six subordinate clauses. Changing the clauses into phrases, we easily reduce it to one matrix clause and two subordinate clauses:

c. Knowing I was ill, the man in the house beside yours came many times to ask if he could do anything for me .

As a matter of fact, there are shades of meaning which have been lost through these processes. For instance, 'if there was anything he could do' differ slightly from 'if he could do anything'. Yet, we have gained greatly in conciseness and pleasantness. The sentence can now run more smoothly. The important facts are made prominent. The gain is much better than the possible loss of meaning.

Here is another example :

98. a. I know she failed in her exam. I have asked for my
    b.   **friend. He is a brilliant student. I want him to teach her.**
    c.   **Because I know she failed in her exam, I have asked for my friend who is a brilliant student so that he might teach her.**
    d.   **Knowing she failed in her exam, I have asked for my friend, a brilliant student, to teach her.**

3.9 Immediate Constituents Analysis

The major contribution of structural grammarians in the field of syntax is their theory of immediate constituents analysis. They maintain that cutting a sentence into its component parts will reveal the basic syntactic relations among those constituents. The method was suggested as a replacement of traditional parsing which structural grammarians revolted against. Here is how such an analysis looks as far as adverbial clauses and phrases of reason are concerned:

99. **I like my master because he is kind.**

100. **I like my master because of his kindness.**

The first cut in any sentence containing a matrix and subordinate clauses is between these two parts. The adverbial clause of reason is cut as any other adverbial. The subordinator is the first element to cut. What remains is a sentence which is, in turn, cut into two parts: a noun phrase functioning as subject and a verb phrase functioning as predicate. In the case of prepositional phrase, the first cut is right after the preposition as in Diagram (2) below:

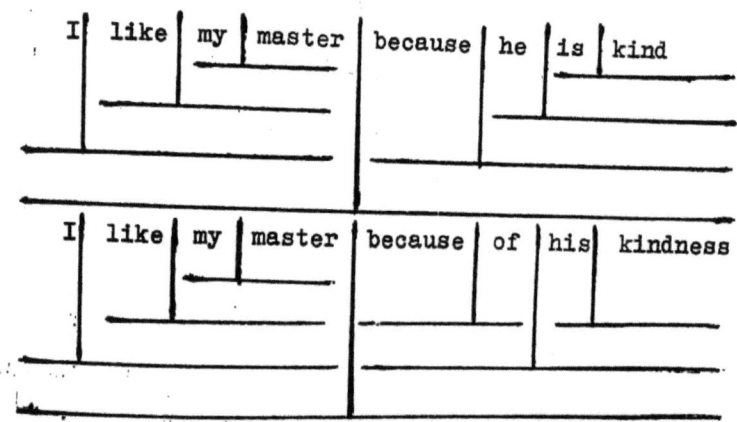

Diagram (2) Analysis of Adverbial Clauses and Phrases of Reason

In general, this analysis is proved to be inadequate at many points and incorrect at certain points because it makes no distinction between clauses of reason and any other clauses. Moreover, it does not account for the variety of meanings, functions and positions that a clause may assume in a sentence. In fact, the whole structural approach to syntax reveals nothing about the nature of a sentence. Therefore, no further discussion of adverbs of reason from the structural point of view will be carried out in the present study.

CHAPTER FOUR

4. Transformational Treatments of Causality

4.1 Some Introductory Remarks

This chapter deals with causality from the transformational point of view. It is concerned mainly with the transformational relationships that hold between kernel sentences, clauses of reason and phrases of identical or similar meaning. That means, an attempt will be made to devise tentative rules that may transform a kernel sentence into an adverbial clause of reason and, when possible, into an adverbial phrase having the same meaning and embed the clause or phrase within a matrix sentence.

4.2 Because and Since Clauses

In chapter three, the concepts of "adjuncts" and "disjuncts" were presented. Now, the major syntactic differences between them will be illustrated by two finite clauses of reasons an adjunct 'because clause' and a disjunct 'since clause':

1.a. Everyone loves Rita because she is so cheerful,

b. Everyone loves Rita since she is so cheerful.

Both clauses can be positioned initially though the 'because clause' usually assumes final position:

2.a. Because she is so cheerful, everyone loves Rita.

b. Since she is so cheerful, everyone loves Rita.

Although these constructions are usually assumed to be equivalent, many grammarians have noted syntactic and, therefore, semantic differences between clauses introduced by **because** and clauses introduced by since.

Goddard (1979 : 206) and Emonds (1976 : 174-175) agree with Quirk et.al (1985 : 1070-1071) that the syntactic differences between the two types of clauses chiefly require focusing devices. Only the 'because clause' can be the focus of a cleft sentence (3), a variant of the pseudo-cleft sentence (4), a question as tested with alternative interrogation (5), a negative as tested with alternative negation (6), and a focusing subjunct such as **<u>only</u>**, **<u>just</u>**, **<u>simply</u>** (7):

3.a.   **It is because she is so cheerful that everyone loves Rita.**

   b.*   **It is since she is so cheerful that everyone loves Rita.**

4. a.   **The reason everyone loves Rita is because she is so cheerful.**

   b.*   **The reason everyone loves Rita is since she is so cheerful.**

5.a.   **Does every one love Rita because she is so cheerful**

        or because she is always helpful ?

   b. *   **Does every one love Pita since she is so cheerful**

        or since she is always helpful ?

6. a.   **Everyone does not love Rita because she is so cheerful but**

        because she is always helpful.

   b.*   **Everyone does not love Rita since she is so cheerful but**

        since she is always helpful.

7.a.   **Everyone loves Rita only because she is so cheerful.**

   b.*   **Everyone loves Rita only since she is so cheerful.**

In addition to all these, a 'since clause' is unacceptable in answer to a why-question:

8.a.   **Why does every one love Rita ? - because she is so cheerful.**

   b.*   **Why does every one love Rita ? - since she is so cheerful.**

On the other hand, Goddard (1979 : 206) notes that "there are also sentences in which 'since clause' is acceptable and 'because' will sound strange or unlikely. He gives the following examples:

9.   **Who do you favour for the Derty, since you have given me such**

good tips, before?

10.   **Since I have to fill in these forms, how much money did you make last forms, how much year ?**

The difference between the 'because clause' and 'since clauses' indicates that the two clause may not have the same deep structures and are, consequently, not transformable into one another , i.e., it is not convenient to devise a rule, that would, for instance, transform a clause beginning with **since** into one beginning with because. This may be due to the fact that **since** has the additional function of a temporal conjunction besides that of causality. It should be kept in mind that clauses with **because** can be reduced into phrases whereas those with **since** cannot.

4.3   Reason Adverbial Clause Transformations

A wide range of structures in English involves embedding. We find embedded sentences in adverbial clauses of reason:

11.   **Suha left the room because Yousif started talking about his wife.**

The transformational processes of embedding always result in a string which is derived from a minimum of two underlying terminal strings one of which is the matrix clause.

In the adverbial clause transformation illustrated Below, the sentences given before the transformation are Kernel sentences which underlie the transformation. The First kernel is the matrix:

12.   **She deserves a reward for some reason. She has done very well this time.**

➡ **She deserves a reward because she has done very well this time.**

Obviously, the rule for the adverbial clause transformation requires that each embedded sentence first be subordinated. This process can easily be accomplished by putting a subordinator before the sentence:

$$S \Longrightarrow Sub + S$$

Subordinating conjunctions are used to join two sentences together. The rule that joins the two sentences, as Lester (1971 s 336) calls it, is the "subordinating conjunction insertion rule".

$$\#S1 \ \#S2 \ \# \Longrightarrow \#S1 + Sub. \ conj + S2\#$$

The subordinator and the following sentence can be moved to the first position in the sentence by the "subordinating conjunction switch rule".

$$S1 + Sub. \ conj + S2 \Longrightarrow Sub. \ conj + S2 + S1$$

13. **Because she has done very well this time, she deserves a reward.**

In a similar manner, Elkins (1974 ; 83) debates that an embedded sentence can be derived by an adverbial clause transformational rule in which one of the deep structure strings signals an appropriate conjunction word as <u>because</u> is signalled by **<u>for some reason</u>** in the following instance:

14. **They respected him much because he had served the firm long and loyally.**

<u>Deep Structure:</u> They respected him much for some reason

T-adv.cl ⟹
He had served the firm long and loyally.
They respected him much because
he had served the firm long and loyally.

The tree Diagram for this sentence looks like following:

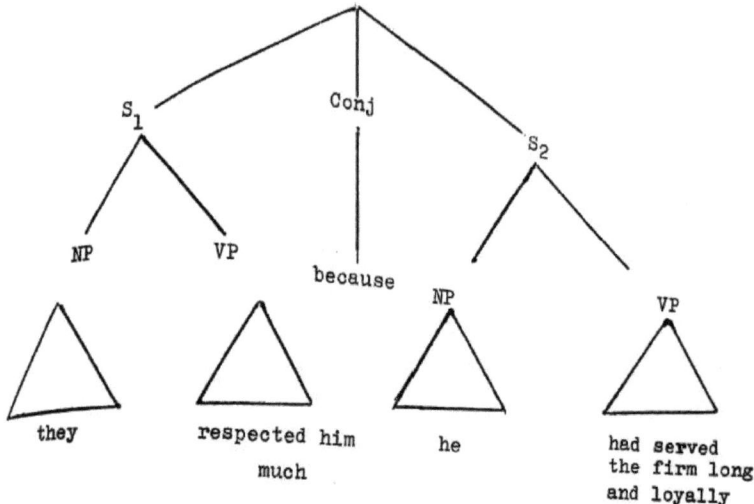

Diagram (3) An Embedded Sentence Derived by an Adverbial Clause Transformational Rule

15.* The officer, because he was mentally tired, was sent to retirement.

In some cases, an embedded sentence is infixed within another as follows:

$$S \longrightarrow S1.a \quad conj. \quad S2 \quad S1.b$$

15. The officer, because he was mentally tired, was sent to retirement.

An abbreviated tree Diagram shows how S1 divides the linguistic elements of S1:

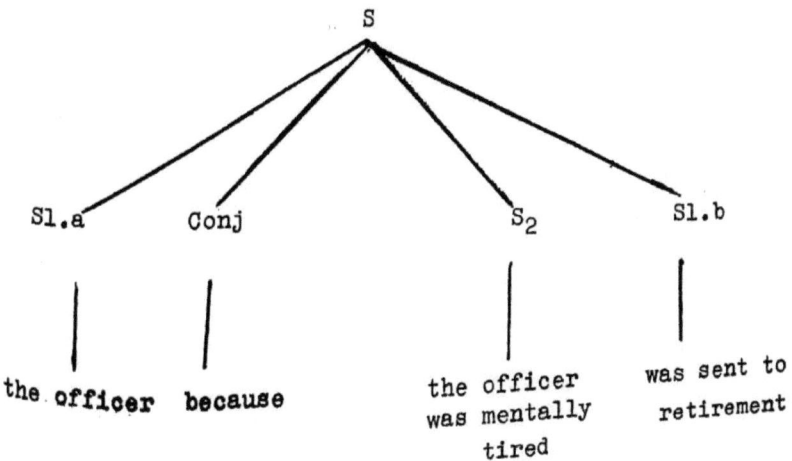

Diagram (4) An Embedded Sentence Infixed within Another

Another point of view hold by Lester is that sentences embedded in certain types of adverb are transformed into subordinating adverb clauses. He (1971: 263-265) distinguishes between sentences embedded as adverbs of reason and condition on the one hand and sentences embedded as adverbs of time and place on the other. The embedded sentences that function as adverbs of reason and condition are introduced by subordinating conjunctions such as because, since, if, unless. These conjunctions do not seem to be internal constituents of the embedded sentences. Such adverbs consist of two subcomponents; a subordinating conjunction and an embedded sentence. The following Diagram might serve to clarify what has already been discussed:

16.   **She failed the exam because she did not study hard enough.**

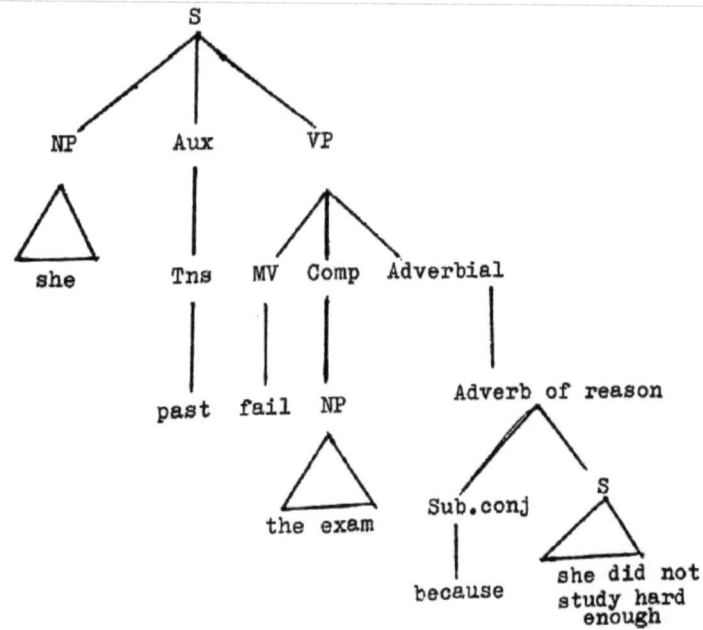

Diagram (5) Sentences Embedded as Adverbs of Reason and Conditions, and of Time and Place

Unlike these, sentences embedded in adverbs of time and place themselves begin with adverbs of time or place. They contain, as part of their own structures, adverbs which are moved to the first position of the embedded sentences by a certain rule called the "adverb switch rule" which can be formalized as follows:

NP + Aux + MV + Comp + Adv ➡ Adv + NP + Aux + MV + Comp

Therefore, such adverbs consist of only one component. That is the sentence. Check Diagram (6) below:

17.   It was midnoon when he flied.

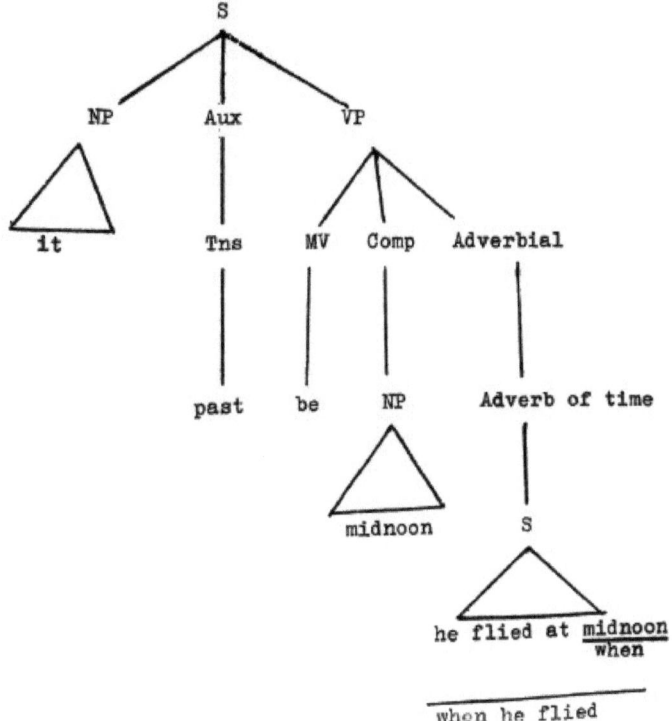

Diagram (6) Adverb Switch Rule

4.4 Participial Phrase Transformations

In performing any transformation, including the participial phrase one, many transformational processes such as deletion, addition, rearrangement, and substitution may occur. Before the application of any transformation, we need to know the structural analysis of the sentence. Examples:

<u>Group -A-</u>

18.　　**He can't work anymore for some reason.**
　　　　He is tired.

T.adv.cl ➡ He can't work anymore because he is tired.

T.pcpl.ph ➡ He can't work anymore because of being tired

T.pcpl.ph ➡ Being tired, he can't work anymore.

19.   I got to my office late for some reason.

I missed the first bus.

T.adv.cl ➡ I got to my office late because I missed

         the first bus.

T.pcpl.ph ➡ I got to my office late because of missing

         the first bus.

T.pcpl.ph ➡ Missing the first bus, I got to my office

         late.

Group —B—

20.   She becomes worried for some reason.

She $\left[\begin{array}{l} \text{has thought} \\ \text{has been thinking} \end{array}\right]$ about the result.

T.adv.cl ➡ She becomes worried because she $\left[\begin{array}{l} \text{has thought} \\ \text{has been thinking} \end{array}\right]$ about the result.

T.pcpl.ph ➡ She becomes worried because of $\left[\begin{array}{l} \text{having thought} \\ \text{thinking} \end{array}\right]$ about the result.

T.pcpl.ph ➡ Having thought about the result, she

becomes worried.

64

21. **He was dismissed for some reason.**

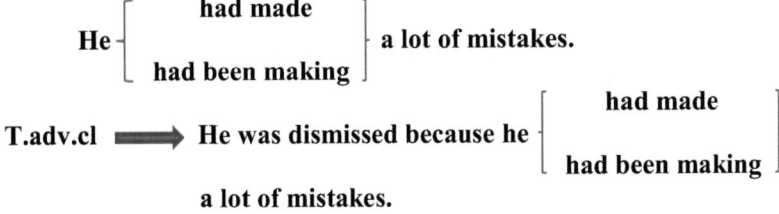

$$\text{He} \left\{ \begin{array}{l} \textbf{had made} \\ \textbf{had been making} \end{array} \right\} \textbf{a lot of mistakes.}$$

T.adv.cl ⟹ He was dismissed because he $\left\{ \begin{array}{l} \textbf{had made} \\ \textbf{had been making} \end{array} \right\}$

a lot of mistakes.

T.pcpl.ph ⟹ He was dismissed because of $\left\{ \begin{array}{l} \textbf{having made} \\ \textbf{making} \end{array} \right\}$

a lot of mistakes.

T.pcpl.ph ⟹ **Having made a lot of mistakes, he was**

dismissed.

The above examples reveal a number of points. First of all, the transformation is performed on the adverbial clause. In all instances, the subject noun phrase is the same in both sentences, i.e., in the matrix and embedded sentences. Accordingly, it is always deleted after applying the phrase transformation. The subordinator may or may not be deleted. The first verb of the transformed verb phrase must end with -ing.

It is noted that the second group of these examples, in contrast with the first one, includes have among its auxiliaries. Consequently, it seems better to present two separate rules for both groups. Considering these points, the rules can be set up in the following manner:

(1)   Sub + NP + Aux + $\left[\begin{array}{l} \textbf{V} \\ \textbf{be} \end{array} \right]$ **+ X** ⟹

$$(\text{Sub}) + \text{ing} + \begin{bmatrix} V \\ be \end{bmatrix} + X$$

$$(2) \quad \text{Sub} + \text{NP} + \text{Aux} + \text{have} + \text{en} + (\text{be} + \text{ing}) + \begin{bmatrix} V \\ be \end{bmatrix} + X \implies$$

$$\begin{bmatrix} \text{Sub} + \begin{bmatrix} \text{ing} + \text{have} + \text{en} \\ \text{ing} \end{bmatrix} \\ \text{ing} + \text{have} + \text{en} \end{bmatrix} + \begin{bmatrix} V \\ be \end{bmatrix} + X$$

In certain situations, the word at expresses the same meaning of because of as the following instances demonstrate:

22.   **She was annoyed at being delayed so long.**

23.   **He was displeased at having been unfairly treated.**

        (because he had been unfairly treated)

24.   **He was annoyed at not having heard from me for a month.**

Two remarks must be made with regard to rule one First» semantic analysis of adverbial participial phrase is complicated by the fact that the participial phrase without a subordinator implies clauses with different meanings. Most commonly, it implies cause and/or time. This remark has been discussed before; a few examples will help to clarify it:

25. Nearing the entrance, X shook hands with my friends.

(As I neared ... , While nearing ...)

26. Considering the difficulties of his position, he has acted admirably.

27. Realizing that Layla was crying, we stopped tormenting her.

What is more, some phrases are preceded by prepositions like on. Although most grammarians hint that such Phrases denote time, yet they may imply causal relation as well:

28. On leaving her, X have felt more relaxed.

29. On hearing the terrible news of his father's death, he fainted.

30. On running very fast, he fell down.

(Since he ran ... , While he was running ...)

Secondly, the first rule can be applied to the following sentences:

31. Since you are active in class, you will certainly pass.

32. My friend failed twice because he was careless.

33. As he was wealthy, All lived in a first-class hotel.

to give :

Group -A-

31. a. Because of being active in class, you will certainly pass.

32. a. My friend failed twice because of being careless.

33. a. Because of being wealthy, All lived in a first-class hotel.

However, this rule can be revised to produce synonymous sentences :

Group -B-

31.b. Because of your activity in class, you will certainly pass.

32.b. My friend failed twice because of his carelessness.

33.b. Because of his wealth, Ali lived in a first-class hotel.

The latter instances (group-B-) are slightly different from the former (group-A-). In group-A, be is retained with **ing** and the result is **being**. The adjective after **being** remains as it is before the transformation. In group-B, the transformational processes are the following: **be** is deleted, a possessive pronoun is added, and a nominalizing suffix such as {{**ness**}, {**dom**}, {**ence**},{ **y**}} is used to nominalize the adjective. Hence, the revised rule will look like the following:

(3)   **Sub + UP + Aux + be + Adj** ⟹
       Sub + Poss. pron + Adj + Nom. suf

Further examples with **because of**, **on account of** and **due to**. (See p . 75).

34.   **The boy won the first prize because of his luck.**

35.   **The thief cannot be caught on account of his quickness.**

36.   **The clerk lost his post due to his dishonesty.**

In certain cases, the conjunction for is used in a way similar to **because of** in the above sentences:

37.   **The teacher punished the boy for disobedience.**

       (... because he was disobedient)

38.   **I forgave him for his rudeness.**

39.   **We praise her for being honest.**

But in such cases, the adjective must be the modifier of the direct object of the sentence which is in turn the subject noun phrase of the embedded sentence.

It is to be noticed that there are a few words which are similar to and interchangeable with **because of**. **On account of** is a more formal alternative to **because of** as an expression of reason. **Owing to** and **due to** could also be used in the same manner. For illustration, all of the following sentences may be obtained from the same deep structure:

40.   **He was unhappy because of his poverty.**

41.   **He was unhappy on account of his poverty.**

42.   **He was unhappy owing to his poverty.**

43.   **He was unhappy due to his poverty.**

English, like most other languages, has ways of giving special emphasis not Just to single words but to entire grammatical units. This emphasis is accomplished by certain transformational rules that invert the normal sentence order to give prominence to certain elements. The cleft sentence inverts the underlying sentence in order to give emphasis to a particular grammatical element. For example, if choose to emphasize the adverbial phrase of reason in the following sentences:

44. The company suffered heavy losses on account of his negligence.

45. She was considered unsuitable for the job due to her lack of experience.

we get:

46. It was on account of his negligence that the company suffered heavy losses.

47. It was due to her lack of experience that she was considered unsuitable for the job.

Owing to is slightly different from the other two due to the presence of the verb **owe ... to ...** Yet, the following sentences can be emphasized in the same manner:

48.   She owed her failure to bad luck.

49.   It was owing to bad luck that she failed.

50.   He owes his present success to his father.

51.   It is owing to his father that he succeeds.

As these examples indicate, this type of inversion transformation moves the element being emphasized (the reason phrase in the above instances) to the first position of the sentence, follows that element by the appropriate relative pronoun (**that** in the examples), and then places **It tense be** in front of the emphasized element, with the tense taken from the tense of the underlying sentence. Formally

69

the rule can be stated as follows:

$$S + Sub + Poss.\ pron. + NP \Longrightarrow It + tense + be +$$
$$Sub + Poss.\ pron. + HP + that + S$$

4.5 Absolute Participial Phrase Transformations

An English sentence may start with a subjectless participial phrase as in the following example :

52.   Having answered the questions, I handed in my paper.

Yet, in certain situations, the participial phrase retains its subject to appear in a new form called an absolute participial phrase, e-g.

53.   John having answered the questions, handed in his paper.

Grammatically, this construction is independent of the sentence with which it is combined. That is, it has absolutely no grammatical connection with the rest of the sentence. This phrase is really a reduction derived from an adverbial clause which functions as a sentence modifier. The well-formedness of the following instances leads to the formation of this construction rule:

<u>Group -A</u>

54.   Since honesty is the best policy, we should be honest.
⟹ Honesty being the best policy, we should be honest.

55.   As he was unable to attend In person, the chairman sent a representative on his behalf.
⟹ The chairman being unable to attend in person, sent a representative on his behalf.

56. Because she has lost the library book, Mary has to pay the fine.

⟹ **Mary having lost the library book, has to pay the fine.**

57. Since the fog had been very dense, no one could see his way.

⟹ **The fog having been very dense, no one could see his way.**

The absolute participial phrase transformation is somehow different from the participial phrase transformation. Whether the subject noun phrases of the matrix and embedded sentences are the same as in (55) and (56) or not as in (54) and (57) does not matter. The subject noun phrase of the embedded sentence is not deleted as in the previous transformation (i.e., participial phrase). Rather, it is moved to the first position of the sentence. The subordinator "hat be omitted. The first word of the transformed verb Phrase should end in -ing. Taking these points into consideration, the rules concerned can be formed as follows.

Rule(4) is for group -A-; rule (5) is for group –B-:

$\qquad$ **(4) Sub + NP + Aux + be +X** ⟹

$\qquad$ **NP + ing + be + X**

$\qquad$ **(5) Sub + NP + Aux + have + en + V + X** ⟹

$\qquad$ **NP + ing + have + en + V + X**

Once more, such phrases usually have implications of cause and/or time. Further examples:

58. $\qquad$ **He being a fool, his friends made him spend a lot on them.**

59. $\qquad$ **Meha being jealous of Dina, struck her.**

60. $\qquad$ **The light having gone out, I went to bed.**

61. $\qquad$ **The performance having ended, immediately every**

$\qquad\qquad$ **one began to talk.**

This device transformation can be used for combining many sentences into one simple sentence as in the following example :

62.   **She left the place. She took her daughter with her.**
           The reason of her going was the unhealthiness of the
           neighbourhood. She was glad to go. They left in the
           afternoon.

➔ **The neighbourhood being unhealthy, she gladly left**

      the place in the afternoon, taking her daughter with her.

Indeed, there are certain structures which are close to this phrase transformation. The following phrases could have the function of non-restrictive postmodifier of 'Albert' Furthermore, they may imply concessive as well as casual relations:

63.   **Albert** $\begin{bmatrix} \text{soon to become a father} \\ \text{sad at the news} \end{bmatrix}$ **travelled abroad**

(Although/Because he was soon to become a father, Albert
      travelled abroad).

Similarly, the phrase "wearing such dark glasses" in the following sentence is subject to a variety of meaningful interpretations:

64.   **The old man, wearing such dark glasses, obviously**
      could not see his proper way clearly.

It could be a reduction of a relative clause 'who was wearing ...' or of a temporal clause such as 'whenever he wore ...or, above all, it could be a reduction of a causal clause 'because he was wearing ...'.

72

4.6 Adverbial Infinitive Phrase Transformations

The close connection between adverbs of reason and purpose has been revealed in the previous chapter. The infinitive phrase can indicate reason as well as purpose. At this stage, we are in a position to derive an infinitive phrase from an adverbial clause. Before formulating the infinitive phrase transformation rule, let us first examine the following examples:

65. **The doctor did his best because he wanted to save the patient.**

   ⟶ **The doctor did his best to save the patient.**

66. **Since he hopes to keep himself fit, he plays table tennis regularly.**

   ⟶ **To keep himself fit, he plays table tennis regularly.**

67. **The poor intended to rob the bank because he wished to be rich overnight.**

   ⟶ **The poor intended to rob the bank to be rich overnight.**

The first requirement which allows this transformation is that the subject of the infinitive phrase must be the same as that of the matrix clause. For example, in (65), it is **the doctor** who did his best and it is **the doctor** himself who wanted to save the patient. **The doctor** is the subject of both **did** and **wanted**. The other condition which allows this transformation is that the adverbial clause of reason should have a verb that expresses a wish or hope such as **want, hope, like, wish, intend, seek,** and **desire** before the infinitive. Otherwise, the transformation is blocked because the new transformed sentence would not make sense.

In carrying out the infinitive phrase transformation, as the above examples indicate, the subordinator is deleted. So is the subject noun phrase of the embedded sentence since it is co-referential with that of the matrix one. The verb used to express the wish of the embedded clause is also deleted. The infinitive alone is retained. All these points considered, the infinitive phrase transformation rule can he formalized in the following way :

(6)   Sub + UP + Aux + V + Inf + X $\longrightarrow$ Inf + X

Further examples :

68.   **Firas takes a walk in the garden to get fresh air.**

69.   **My uncle has saved much money to have a house built.**

70.   **That girl wears glasses to make people think she is well-educated.**

When infinitive clauses are coordinated, they can be transformed in the same manner:

71.   **I visited Paris because I wanted to observe the people and I wanted to study their customs.**

$\longrightarrow$ **I visited Paris to observe the people and to study their customs.**

72.   **She works hard because she wants to pass in the first division and she hopes to win a scholarship.**

$\longrightarrow$ **She works hard to pass in the first division and to win a scholarship.**

73.   **The dean called a meeting because he wanted to discuss the problem of college discipline and he would like to know the final preparation of the annual meeting.**

$\longrightarrow$ **The dean called a meeting to discuss the problem of college discipline and to know the final preparation of the annual meeting.**

The following sentences in (74) can be put together in one sentence showing the participial phrase transformation discussed earlier and the infinitive phrase transformation under discussion:

74.   **Mary turned on the TV. She did not see anything worth watching. She went next door. She wanted to see Jane. She would like to have a chat.**

⟶   **Not seeing anything worth watching on the TV., Mary went next door to see Jane and to have a chat.**

On the other hand, the infinitive can be used in certain cases to express the cause with its result. Clauses of result are constructed by using **so... that** or **such ... that**. What precedes that indicates the reason whereas what follows it denotes the result. The following illustrations might help to make matters clear:

75.   **I was so excited that I could not think.**
⟶   **I was too excited to think.**
76.   **This is so dear we cannot buy it.**
⟶   **This is too dear to buy.**
77.   **The coffee was so hot that he could not drink it**
⟶   **The coffee was too hot for him to drink.**

The following paraphrases of the above sentences demonstrate clearly the causal relation in terms of reason clauses:

78.   **I could not think because I was too excited.**
79.   **We cannot buy this because it is too dear.**
80.   **He could not drink the coffee because it was too hot.**

It has to be mentioned that **so** goes with an adjective standing without a noun or with an adverb. When there is a noun with the adjective, <u>such</u> is used. However, <u>**so**</u> may be used in a sentence of this kind but if it comes so, the adjective must follow <u>**so**</u> immediately:

81.   **he is so fat that he cannot get through the door.**

82.   **He is such a fat man that he cannot get through the door.**

83.   **He is so fat a man that he cannot get through the door.**

All these se sentences can be transformed in the same manner:

➡ **He is too fat to get through the door.**

This may be paraphrased as:

84.   **He cannot get through the door because he is too fat.**

The following phrases are a mixture of participial and infinitive phrases:

85.   **Finding that the suit was too expensive to buy, Paul decided to buy a pair of shoes instead.**

86.   **Realizing that the Problem is too difficult for her to solve, Betty consults her father.**

4.7 Some Other Transformations

<u>4.7.1</u> **The adverbial clauses in the following examples have the features:**

$$Sub + NP^2 + Aux + Be + Adj$$

87.   **They died because the food was poisonous.**

88.   **She was dismissed because her behaviour was bad.**

89.   **The horrible accident took place because the bridge was narrow.**

Such clauses could be changed into phrases by another transformation rule if certain points are taken into account. Firstly, the subject noun phrase of the embedded adverbial clause (NP^2) is not the same as that of the matrix. Secondly, the verb <u>be</u> is the main verb of the embedded Sentence. Thirdly, the adjective should be of the attributive type, i.e., it can occur before the noun it modifies so that it can undergo the following transformation:

$$NP + be + Adj \longrightarrow Adj + NP$$

The boy is clever $\longrightarrow$ **the clever boy**

Otherwise, if the adjective is predicative, this transformation is blocked because it will result in an unacceptable sentence. This comes from the fact that there are a few English adjectives that cannot occur in a pronominal position. These include: <u>afraid</u>, <u>ashamed</u>. <u>aware</u>, <u>aghast</u>. <u>ablaze</u>, <u>alive</u> and others:

The boy is still alive $\longrightarrow$ *** the alive boy**

If all the above conditions are observed and applied, sentences 87, 88 and 89 above will be transformed into 87.a, 88.a and 89.a respectively:

87.   a.   **They died because of the poisonous food.**

88.   a.   **She was dismissed due to her bad behaviour.**

89.   a.   **The horrible accident took place owing to the narrow bridge.**

What happens really is a matter of rearrangement and deletion. Thus, the rule will be' as follows:

(7)   **Sub + NP^2 + Aux + be + Adj** $\Longrightarrow$

Sub + Det + Adj + NP^2

It is to be mentioned that the transformed sentences above may come in another form but this is not very common:

87.   **b. They died because of the food being poisonous.**
88.   **b. She was dismissed because of her behavior being bad.**
89.   **b. The horrible accident took place because of the bridge being narrow.**

Further examples:
90.   **It may rain today on account of the cloudy sky.**
91.   **Because of the fine weather and the cheap food, they resolved to stay at the inn another night.**
92.   **She was crying because of the news being sad.**

On the other hand, in many other instances, a noun in the "-s" or "of-" genitive case may be used in reason transformation:

93.   **I spent most of my holiday at home because of my father's illness. (because of the illness of my father)**
94.   **The maxi's life was saved owing to the doctor's skill.**
95.   **The republic was saved because of the commander's quick thinking. (because the commander was quick to think)**
96.   **The school was closed due to an outbreak of measles. (because measles had broken out)**
97.   **The accident happened because of the failure of brake. (because the brake failed)**

4.7.2 **In some constructions in English, the sentences with phrase transformations sound much better than the sentences with the adverbial clauses. Such phrases sometimes seem to be derived from a "there insertion"**

which is deleted in the transformation. Only the subordinator and one or two words remain. Here are some examples:

98. The plane did not fly because there was a storm.

➡ The plane did not fly because of a storm.

99. We came late because there was an accident.

➡ We came late due to an accident.

100. They can't travel abroad because there is a war.

➡ They can't travel abroad owing to a war.

101. They put off the trip because there is rain.

➡ They put off the trip on account of rain.

Such transformation have a rule like the following:

(8)   Sub + there + Aux + be + NP ➡ Sub + NP

Yet, there are similar sentences which this rule may not apply to:

102. Ahmed could not treat his friends because of the cost.

103. He was given Preference on account of his name.

104. I could not see my way because of darkness.

105. The accident took place owing to speed.

4.8 Ambiguity

In some cases, modifying reason phrases create ambiguity. Gabbay and Moravcsik (1979 : 254) illustrate this ambiguity through the following sentence:

106. He does not wear a jacket because of the weather.

We need not generate two syntactic analysis for this sentence. Roughly, the structure is illustrated in Diagram (7) below:

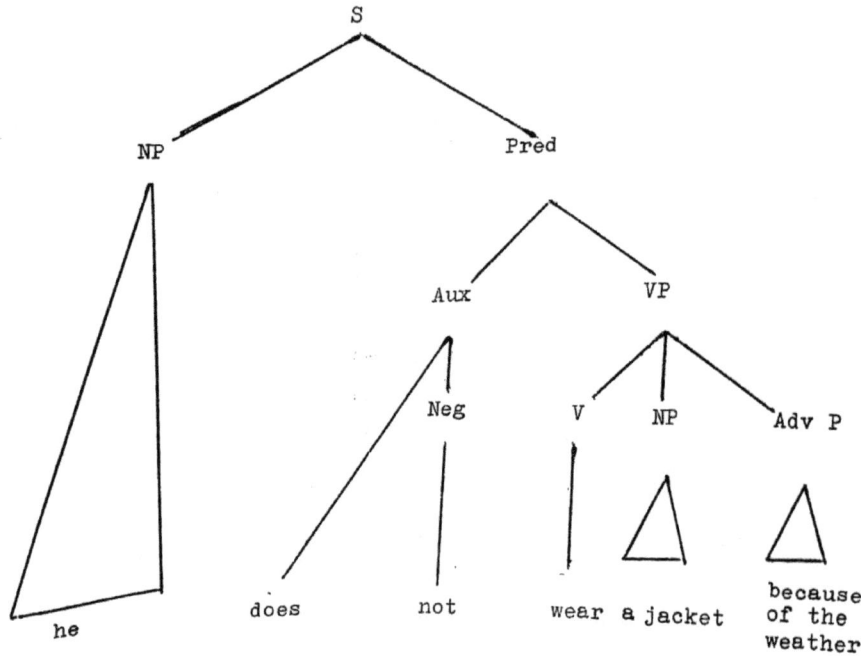

Diagram (7) Reason Phrases Ambiguity

This syntactic analysis has two semantic interpretations:

106.   **a. He does not [(wear a jacket) because of the weather.]**

b. He wears a jacket not (because of the weather).

That means, in (106.a), he does something else because of the weather. In (106.b), the 'because clause' modifies only the verb phrase, and the scope of the negation is the bracketed material.

This example brings out that the negative sentence with an adverbial has typically the modifying element, i.e., the adverbial negated. When the adverb is negated,) the negative and the element negated are not adjacent syntactic units. This can be handled on the semantic level by a semantic transformation rather than on the syntactic level.

To take another example, consider the following question:

107.   Does he beat his sister because he does not like her ?

This sentence implies that he beats his sister and is questioning his reason for doing so. It is synonymous with:

108.   Is it because he does not like her that he beats his sister?

Lakoff (1970: 169) points out that a sentence like the following:

109.   He does not beat his sister because he likes her.

has two senses which are synonymous with:

110.   It is because he likes her that he does not beat his sister.

111.   It is not because he likes her that he beats his sister.

Lakoff (1970 : 183) remarks that in sentences with more than one adverbial, a change in the order of the adverbials may produce a considerable change in the meaning of the sentence. For instance, consider:

112.   He beats his sister often because she is careless.

113.   He often beats his sister because she is careless.

In (112), he is telling the reason why he heats his sister often. In (113), he is telling the frequency with which Heats his sister because she is careless. The following corresponding questions reveal this distinction quite Nearly:

114.   Does he beat his sister often because she is careless?

115.   Does he often beat his sister because she is careless?

Similarly, (114) assumes that he beats his sister often is questioning his reason for doing so. Whereas (115) assumes that he beats his sister because she is careless and is questioning how often he does so.

On the other hand, adverbial clauses of reason may be embedded between two adverbials. For Smith and Wilson (1980 : 46), a sentence like the following is unacceptable in most contexts because of its extreme syntactic complexity:

116. **If because when Nada came in Firas left Suha cried,**
I would be surprised.

On closer examination, it is possible to see that it is regularly formed according to the standard principles of English. That is, the structure of the sentence is as follows:

If A happened, I'd be surprised
A : Because B happened, Suha cried
B : When Nada came in, Firas left

However, the syntactic complexity of the sentence arises from the difficulty in unraveling its message.

CHAPTER FIVE

5. Conclusions and Suggestions

5.1 Summary and Conclusions

In order to give a fairly systematic presentation of the topic in question, we need to state the following points and conclusions:

(1) The causal principle is so central to, all kinds of knowledge that it is deeply embedded in every science. This is obvious in assuming that every event has a cause although there is no philosophical or scientific way of proving this notion. Philosophers think that we are always after causes behind every event. For example , law would be quite meaningless if men were not asked to investigate the causes of different unwanted events such as death, crime, war, disease and others. Likewise, undoubtedly, the battle against malaria begins with the search for its cause and then measures are taken to eliminate that cause or moderate its effect.

(2) In their definitions of causal statements, philosophers, logicians, and grammarians generally agree that there are two events or states: cause and effect or result. While the subordinate clause expresses the cause of the event, the matrix clause expresses the effect. The former determines and depends on the latter. Thus, the connection between cause and effect is necessary. This connection is one of the means or conditions which some philosophers put in determining the concept of causation.

(3) Causal relationships appear in various forms, positions, and orders. Clauses of reason are most commonly introduced by **because, since, as**, and **for**. Of these conjunctions, **because** seems to denote the closest causal relations; **as** the weakest; **since** and **for** respectively come between. The difference between them is chiefly a difference in emphasis. 'Because clause' has a tendency to follow the matrix clause and has the result-reason order whereas 'as and since clauses' have a tendency to precede it and have the consequence of reason-result. **For** stands on the gradient between the pure coordinator and the pure subordinator. It has a syntactic peculiarity not shared by any of the above conjunctions; it must always stand between the two elements joined. Since **for**, unlike other coordinators, never connects anything but clauses, grammarians are often dubious about calling it a coordinating conjunction. The following examples may help to clarify this distinction:

1. **The policeman gave the lady a ticket because she crossed the street against the traffic signal.**
2. **Since (As) it is a holiday today, all offices are closed.**
3. **You must start early for you have many things to do.**

In addition to this, the following sequence reflects a causal relation between two sentences with no connection. The reason or explanation of the first sentence is given in the second:

4. **She phoned the police; she had heard an explosion.**

The instances below are some of the various ways that demonstrate causality:

5. **The cause of the chemical change is the high temperature.**
6. **She was annoyed at being rebuked.**
7. **He refuses to be in any one's debt. That is why you cannot help him.**
8. **Happy, because her father was at home, she talked about her nice birthday celebration.**

(4) The differences between the major cause subordinators discussed above lead to the following point. Of the three grammatical categories: adjunct, disjunct, and

conjunct, it is only the adjuncts that closely resemble other sentence elements like subject, object, and complement. Because clauses and phrases1 are close to adjuncts while other clauses or phrases of reason are like disjuncts. This comes from the ability of adjuncts to be the focus of a cleft sentence:

9.   **Lyons was universally respected because of his virtue.**

10.   **It was Lyons wh0 was universally respected because of his virtue. (subject)**

11.   **It was because of his virtue that Lyons was universally respected. (adjunct)**

The parallels extend also to contrast in alternative negation and interrogation and in being the focus of focusing subjuncts.

12.   **Lyons was not universally respected because of his virtue but (he was universally respected) because of his wisdom.**

13.   **Was Lyons universally respected because of his virtue or (was he universally respected) because of his wisdom ?**

14.   **Lyons was universally respected simply because of his virtue.**

On the other hand, disjuncts and conjucts are not capable of occurring in those positions. They would be unacceptable there.

(5) In certain cases, the relation between reason and time has to be inferred when it is expressed by certain subordinators like <u>**since**</u> and <u>**as**</u> and by participial and absolute participial phrases. The reason behind this is   that such structures might indicate both the causal and temporal relations. Consequently, ambiguity may sometimes arise. In short, the relation is more semantic than syntactic because the difficulty is how to find the range of semantic realization and connection which subordinate clauses may bear to the matrix clause when no subordinator is present. Illustrations include:

15. As the guest stayed too long, he was .unwelcomed.
16. Realizing his mistakes, he ran for help.
17. Maradona being unable to play, the team lost the match.

(6) There are certain affinities between clauses of reason and other clauses. While the same question can be answered in different ways showing the reason and purpose, as this has been observed previously, the relation between clauses of reason and those of result and conjunct such as **so ... that**, **therefore**, and **consequently** is another story. The type of this relation is an inversion of the two clauses or sentences with a subordinator of reason between them.

For instance:

18. Professor Allen has been teaching such a long time
    that he is a little tired.
19. Professor Allen is a little because he has been teaching such a
    long time.
20. The final exam is approaching, so they have put off the trip.
21. They have put off the trip because the final exam is approaching,

(7) Since the meanings indicated by clauses and phrases of reason are almost identical, the present study has attempted to suggest some tentative transformational rules which link these phrases and clauses (surface structures) to the same deep structure. Before the application of any transformation ., however, there are certain common conditions to be noted. First of all, the transformation is carried out on the adverbial clause. Since reason clauses consist of two sentences conjoined by a subordinator, the subject noun phrase of the embedded sentence, i.e., of the sentence containing the reason clause, should be checked to find whether it is the same as or different from that of the matrix sentence. The verb phrase of the embedded sentence has to be examined also; whether it consists of be, have, a verb that expresses a wish, or any other verb. The kind of adjective that follows be as a main verb has to be considered too. The reason for these conditions is that in each case certain transformational rules are applicable. Such conditions, of course, involve many transformational processes, particularly deletion and rearrangement.

(8) Considering the conditions of every rule discussed in chapter four, these rules could be summed up as follows:

$$\textbf{(1) Sub + NP + Aux +} \begin{bmatrix} \textbf{v} \\ \textbf{be} \end{bmatrix} \textbf{+ X} \implies \textbf{(Sub) + ing +} \begin{bmatrix} \textbf{v} \\ \textbf{be} \end{bmatrix} \textbf{+ X}$$

22. **Majid usually gets good grades because he studies very hard.**

⟹ **Majid usually gets good grades very hard.**

$$\textbf{(2) Sub + NP + Aux + have + en + (be + ing) +} \begin{bmatrix} \textbf{v} \\ \textbf{be} \end{bmatrix} \textbf{+ X} \implies$$

$$\begin{bmatrix} \textbf{Sub} & \begin{bmatrix} \textbf{ing + have + en} \\ \textbf{ing} \\ \textbf{ing + have + en} \end{bmatrix} \end{bmatrix} + \begin{bmatrix} \textbf{v} \\ \textbf{be} \end{bmatrix} + \textbf{ing}$$

23. **He must have seen the accident because he had been at the scene.**
⟹ **He must have seen the accident because of having been at the scene.**

(3) **Sub + NP + Aux + be + Adj.** ⟹
Sub + Poss. pron. +Adj. + Nom Suf.

24. She does not look cheerful because she is ill.

➡ She does not look cheerful on account of her illness.

(4) Sub + NP + Aux + be + X ➡ NP + ing + be + X

25. Since dinner was ready, my wife called me to the table.

➡ Dinner being ready, my wife called me to the table.

(5) Sub + NP + Aux + have + en + v + x ➡

NP + ing + have + en + v + x

26. As the game had ended all the spectators left the playground.

➡ The game having ended, all the spectators left the playground.

(6) Sub + NP + Aux + v + inf. + X ➡ inf. + v

27. The soldier sacrified himself because he wished to save his
friend.

➡ The soldier sacrified himself to save his friend.

(7) Sub + NP^2 + Aux + be + Adj. ➡ Sub + Det. + Adj. +NP^2

28. We decide to spend the summer holiday in the north
of Iraq because the weather is fine.

➡ We decide to spend the summer holiday in the north
of Iraq due to the fine weather.

(8) Sub + there + Aux + be + NP ➡ Sub + NP

29. I cannot study well because there is noise.

➡ I cannot study well owing to noise.

Traditionally speaking, if the sentence is divided into simple, complex, and compound, the conjunctions used with each type is as illustrated in Diagram (8) below:

Complex	Simple	Compound
because, since, as	because of, due to owing to, on account of	for

Diagram (8) The Conjunctions used with Complex, simple and Compound Sentences

Examples:

30. The sentence is rejected because it is ungrammatical.

31. The sentence is rejected because of ungrammaticality.

32. The sentence is rejected for it is ungrammatical.

5.2 Suggestions for Further Research

The very most striking feature to be noted in this study seems to be the great wealth of causal expressions. Since this study is limited mainly to adverbial clauses and phrases of reason, what remains is great. Causative constructions like the following could make good topics for other studies.

33.   He gets them to correct the mistakes.

34.   She has (makes) her pupils prepare questions.

It is worth mentioning that most studies have concerned themselves with levels of language that never go beyond the simple or basic sentence. Therefore, the study of how to change a complex sentence with more than one finite verb into a simple sentence, i.e., with one finite verb without changing the basic meaning of the sentence might be a remarkable topic* This topic includes adverbial clauses of time, purpose, result, concession, condition, and others. In these studies, attempts could be made to devise tentative rules. Moreover, exceptions of the rules, including those exceptions of reason in this study, could be collected and if possible rules for them are produced. In particular, adverbial, clauses of result might be a distinguished subject for a further research.

BIBLIOGRAPHY

Allen, W. Standard. 1971 Living English Structure London : Hazell Watson and Uiney Ltd.

Altenberg, B. 1984 "Causal Linking in Spoken and Written English" in Studia Linguistica pp. 20-69.

Barrett, Clifford 1959. **Philosophy** . New York :The Macmillan Company.

Bartsch, Renate (tran.) 1976. **The Grammar of Adverbials**. Amsterdaum: North Holland Publishing Company.

Campbell, R.R. 1962. **English Composition for Foreign Students**. Hong Kong: Peninsula Press Ltd.

Chander, Kailash and Ranchan, Indu 1986. Vikas Book of English Grammar, Composition and Translation. Vol. II.India: Sanjay Printers, Shahadra, Delhi.

Chandra,Harish and Sing, Dalin 1974. Vikas Book of General English. India: Konark Printers, Lakshmi Nagar, Delhi.

Copleston, Frederick S.J. 1964. A History of Philosophy Vol. 5. Modern Philosophy : The British Philosophers. P.II. Berkeley to Hume. New York: The Newman Press and Burns & Oates, Ltd.

Drummond, Gordon. 1975. **English Structure Practice**. London: Longman Group Ltd.

Eckersley, C.E. and Eckersley, J.M. 1963. **A Comprehensive English Grammar for Foreign Students**. Hong Kong: The Continental Printing Co. Ltd.

Elkins, William R. 1974. **A New English Primer**. New York: St. Martin's Press. Inc.

Emonds, Joseph E. 1976. **A Transformational Approach to English Syntax**. New York , Academic Press, Inc.

Flew, Antony 1979. **A Dictionary of Philosophy**. London : Richard Clay (The Chaucer Press) Ltd.

Foster, John 1985. A.J. Ayer. London : Thetford Press.

Frank, Marcella 1972. **Modern English**. London: Prentice-Hall, Inc.

Gabbay, Dov. M. and Moravcsik, Julivs M. 1979. "Negation and Denial" in Studies in Formal Semantics (ed.) Guenthner, Franz and Rohrew, Christian. Amsterdaum: North-Holland Publishing Company.

Gleason, H.A. Jr. 1965. **Linguistics and English Grammar**. New York : Holt, Rinehart andWinston, Inc.

Goddard, Cliff (ed.) 1979. "Particles and Illocutionary Semantics" in Papers in Linguistic. Vol. 12 . p. 1-2.pp. 185-231.

Gove, P. B. et. Al 1961. Webster's Third New International Dictionary. London: G.C. Merrian Co.

Greenbaum, Sidney. 1969. **Studies in English Adverbial Usage**. London: William Clowes and Sons Ltd.

Hammond, Robert 1947. The Philosophy of Al-Farabi and its Influence on Medieval Thought. New York: The Hobson Book Press.

Hook, J.N. and Mathews, E.G. 1956. **Modern American Grammar and Usage**. New York : The Ronald Press Company.

Hossack, A. 1979. **The Essence of Precis**. London : Cox Wyman Ltd.

House, Homer C. and Harman, Susan Emolyn 1950. **Descriptive English Grammar**. New York: Prentice-Hall, Inc.

Huddleston, Rodney. 1984. **Introduction to the Grammar of English**. London: Cambridge University Press.

Hutchins, Robert Maynard 1952. The Great Ideas. A Syntopicon of Great Books of the Western World. Vol. 1 New York: The University of Chicago Press.

Jepson, R.W. 1939. **An Outline English Grammar**. London : Ballantyne Press.

Jesperson, Otto. 1952. **Essentials of English Grammar**. London: Morrison and Gibb Ltd.

.... 1970. **A Modern English Grammar P.V. Syntax**. London: George Allen & Unwin Ltd.

Kench, A.B. 1981. **Essential Grammar Practice**. Hong Kong: The Macmillan Press, Ltd.

Korner, Stephan 1986. "On Some Methods and Results of Philosophical Analysis" in Philosophy in Britain Today (ed.) Shanker, S.G. London: Mackays of Chatham Ltd.

Lakoff, George 1970. **Irregularity in Syntax**. New York : Holt, Rinehart and Winston, Inc.

Lester, Mark 1971. **Introductory Transformational Grammar of English**. New York : Holt, Rinehart and Winston Inc.

Lewis, B. et.al 1966. **The Encyclopedia of Islam**. Vol. III. s.v "Allah".

Marcus, Marie 1977. **Diagnostic Teaching of Language Arts**. New York: John Wiley & Sons, Inc.

Morreall, John. 1979 "The Evidential Use of Because" in Papers in Linguistics. Vol. 12. p. 1-2. pp. 231-238.

Nasar, Seyyed Hossein 1964. **An Introduction to Islamic Cosmological Doctorines**. New York: Harvard University Press.

Nesfield, J.C. 1947. **Modern English Grammar**. London: Macmillan and Company ltd.

Quinn, P.J. (comp.) 1963. **Comprehension Precis and Grammar**. London: Collins Press.

Quirk, R. et.al 1972. **A Grammar of Contemporary English**. London: Longman Group Ltd.

...............................1985. **A Comprehensive Grammar of the English Language**. London. Longman Group Ltd.

Roberts, Paul 1954. **Understanding Grammar**. New York: Harper & Row, Publishers, Inc.

.........................1956. **Patterns of English**. New York: Harcourt, Brace & World, Inc.

Rosenthal, M. and Yudin, P. (eds.) 1967. **A Dictionary of Philosophy**. Moscow: Progress Publisher.

Russell, Bertrand. 1948. **History of Western Philosophy**. London: Unwin Brothers Ltd.

.........................1968. **The Analysis of Mind**. London: Unwin Brothers Ltd.

.........................1970. **An Outline of Philosophy**. London : C. Tinling and Co. Ltd.

Schibsbye, Knud. 1965. **A Modern English of Grammar**. London : Oxford University Press.

Schuster, Edger H. 1965. **Grammar, Usage, and Style**. New York: McGraw-Hill, Inc.

Smith, Neil and Wilson, Deirdre 1980. Modern Linguistics: The Result of Chomsky's Revolution. London: Richard Clay (The Chaucer Press) Ltd.

Stace, W.T. 1962. **A Critical History of Greek Philosophy**. London: Macmillan and Company Ltd.

Stumpf, Samuel Enoch 1983. **Philosophy**. History and Problems. New York: McGraw-Hill, Inc.

Taylor, Richard 1967. **The Encyclopedia of Philosophy**. Vol. II. s.v. "causation".

Thomson, A. J. and Martinet, A.V. 1973. **A Practical English Grammar**. London : Oxford University Press.

Tipping, L. 1961. **Matriculation English Grammar of Modern English Usage**. London: Macmillian and Company Ltd.

Tregidge, P.S. 1981. **English Grammar in Practice**. London: Richard Clay (The Chaucer Press) Ltd.

Wren, P.C. and Martin, H. 1985. **High School English Grammar and Composition**. New Delhi Chand & Company Ltd.

Zandvoort, R. W. 1977. **A Handbook of English Grammar**. Hong Kong , Wing Tax Cheung Printing Co. Ltd.